GLOBETROTTER™

M

AND GOA

Robin Gauldie

NEW HOLLAND

NEW HOLLAND

★★★ Highly recommended
★★ Recommended
★ See if you can

Sixth edition published in 2015
by MapStudio™
10 9 8 7 6 5 4 3 2 1
www.globetrottertravelguides.com

Distributed in Africa by
MapStudio™
Unit3, Block B, M5 Park, Eastman Road,
Maitland 7405, Cape Town, South Africa
PO Box 193, Maitland 7404

Distributed in the UK/Europe/Asia by
John Beaufoy Publishing Ltd

Distributed in the USA by
National Book Network

ISBN 978 1 77026 681 0

Commissioning Editor: Elaine Fick
DTP Cartographic Manager: Genené Hart
Editors: Elaine Fick, Thea Grobbelaar, Lorissa Bouwer, Mary Duncan, Sean Fraser, Susannah Coucher
Design and DTP: Nicole Bannister, Kathryn Fotheringham
Cartographers: Rudi de Lange, Reneé Spocter, Lorissa Bouwer, Marisa Roman, Desirée Oosterberg
Picture Researcher: Shavonne Govender

Reproduction by Hirt & Carter (Pty) Ltd, Cape Town
Printed and bound by Craft Print International Ltd, Singapore

Photographic Credits:
Nick Laing/awl-images.com; Jeanetta Baker (PhotoBank), page 17; Geoff Benson, page 92; Mark Boekstein, page 7; Gerald Cubitt, title page, pages 11, 19, 26, 62, 67, 68, 70, 76, 93, 108, 119 (bottom); FootPrints, page 35; Cecilia Innes, page 15, 46; LifeFile, pages 24, 25, 28, 48, 82, 85, 86, 89, 91, 99, 102, 106 (top), 112, 113, 120; The Mansell Collection, pages 13, 16; Neil McAllister, 8, 12, 27, 80, 105; PictureBank, pages 4, 9, 37, 87, 111; Simon Reddy, pages 51, 59, 88, 110; Shutterstock, pages, 20, 30, 33, 40, 44, 45, 52, 56, 61, 65, 75, 77, 79, 96, 100, 116; Travel Pictures Ltd, cover, page 22.

Keep us current
Information in travel guides is apt to change, which is why we regularly update our guides. We'd be grateful to receive feedback if you've noted something we should include in our updates. If you have new information, please share it with us by writing to the Commissioning Editor at the MapStudio address on this page. The most significant contribution to each new edition will receive a free copy of the updated guide.

Front Cover: *Temple at the southermost point of India, Kanniyakumari, Tamil Nadu.*
Title Page: *Sari-clad women at sunset.*

CONTENTS

1
Introducing Mumbai and Goa

The throbbing megalopolis of Mumbai is guaranteed to amaze even the most blase visitor. An estimated 22 million people live in this vast urban sprawl, making it one of the 21st century's largest conurbations. Almost 10 million live in some of the world's most appalling slums, while the city's new elite revel in conspicuous luxury. In between, a recently prosperous middle class enjoys such perks as private cars, air-conditioned homes, smartphones and broadband access.

Goa, India's smallest state, is utterly different. Its centuries-old Portuguese heritage sets it apart from the rest of India, and its mellow climate and its Arabian Sea beaches have made it a favourite with holidaymakers from backpackers on a shoe-string to those seeking ultimate luxury.

But Goa has far more to offer than the average beach resort. Golden sands, winter sunshine, superb seafood and low prices are the most obvious of its charms. An older, more exotic India exists side by side with the swimming pools and golf courses of Goa's modern hotels; an India where sacred cows amble down village roads, where fishermen haul their boats up onto beaches beside sunbathing tourists and where villagers drive ox-drawn ploughs through muddy rice-fields in the shadow of holiday hotels. Compared with many other parts of India, Goa inflicts relatively little culture shock on the visitor experiencing the wonders and worries of the developing world for the first time. Certainly, most Goans do not enjoy the standard of living most Westerners take for granted but there is little of the destitution which blights the streets of less fortunate regions of the Indian subcontinent.

Top Attractions

*** **Old Goa:** spectacular ruins of the first 16th-century Portuguese colonial capital.
*** **Panaji:** sleepy Portuguese-built town, Goa's state capital.
*** **Anjuna:** superb beach and cheerful village with a colourful weekly market.
*** **Aguada:** top beach for luxury resort hotels.
** **Colva-Benaulim:** Goa's longest, finest, least crowded beaches.

◀ *Opposite: Colva Beach is one of the finest in southern Goa, with miles of clean sand.*

▶ *Right: coconut palms, like these growing near Chapora, are an important crop plant.*

during the summer months. The best time of year to visit is between the middle of September and the end of February when daytime temperatures average around 27°C (80°F) with seven to nine hours of sunshine per day.

At this time of year, **humidity** is quite low and night-time temperatures are cooler. From early March, the temperature starts to climb, and can rise as high as 35°C (95°F) in April and May. The **monsoon**, which begins in June, comes as a relief for local people after the hot, dry months of early summer, bringing welcome rain and lower temperatures. Goa can be at its most beautiful at this time of year, with the vivid green of newly sprouting rice in place of the bare red earth and parched vegetation of the dry season. Cloudy skies and heavy rain, however, are a powerful deterrent to most visitors. **Rainfall** is at its heaviest in July when Goa receives up to 90cm (36in) of rain in a single month. Travelling within

GOA	J	F	M	A	M	J	J	A	S	O	N	D
AVERAGE TEMP. °C	25	26	27	29	30	28	26	26	26	27	27	27
AVERAGE TEMP. °F	76	77	78	84	85	84	77	77	77	78	78	78
DAYS OF RAINFALL	1	0	1	8	9	30	30	30	20	10	5	5
RAINFALL mm	2	0	4	17	18	500	890	340	277	122	20	30
RAINFALL in	-	-	.15	.9	.9	20	36	14	11	5	.1	1.2

India generally becomes more difficult during the rainy season and Goa is no exception. Road, rail and air travel schedules are prone to disruption. Strong winds and high seas also put most beaches off limits at this time of year. The rains slacken off through August and draw to an end in early to mid-September.

The other destinations in this guide have slightly different weather patterns. **Mumbai** has a similar monsoon season, but is hotter all year round than Goa, with average maximum temperatures only dipping below 30°C (85°F) in August. Inland, **Maharashtra** is drier with cooler weather at higher altitudes. Coastal **Kerala** experiences the same weather pattern as Goa, but the high inland plateau of **Karnataka** escapes the heaviest monsoon rains and has slightly cooler day and night temperatures.

Temple Monkeys

Flocks of mischievous **macaque monkeys** inhabit many Indian temple precincts, especially those sacred to **Hanuman**, the monkey-god. They are usually harmless, but they may sometimes make a grab for a dangling bag or camera. Feeding them is not advisable, as they may bite.

Plant Life

At least 3000 years of human settlement, intensive farming, and a fast-growing population mean much of Goa's landscape is man-made, leaving little space for large wild animals. Around the coast and tourist resort areas, almost

◀ *Left: Much of Goa is covered by rice fields.*

Holy Cows

All over India, small flocks of white **cattle** amble freely through the streets, browse on patches of wasteland or stroll along the beach. According to Hindu custom, these sacred cows and bulls may not be harmed. Even the bulls are harmless, with none of the aggressive instincts of European bullocks, but sacred cattle are a frequent obstruction to traffic.

all the land is under cultivation with **crops** such as **coconut** and **cashew**, **mango**, **pineapple** and **rice** pushing out the wild flowers. Many of the brilliant **flowers** which brighten the gardens and balconies of Goanese homes and resorts are imports, such as the scarlet and purple bougainvillea, originally from Brazil, which flourishes everywhere. Most visitors arrive during the dry winter months, when anything which is not irrigated dies, and so miss the explosion of flowers and greenery which greets the first monsoon rains when they fall in June.

Wildlife

Birds and **butterflies** fare better than wild mammals. Gorgeously coloured butterflies float around hotel gardens, and palm plantations and flooded rice paddies attract many species of birds. Goa's bird life is far too rich to list in detail here, but the most easily spotted include **white herons**, **cattle egrets** and other wading birds which stalk fish and frogs among the sprouting rice. Goa has at least five species of **kingfisher**, which are often seen perching on telephone wires overlooking rice fields. **Bee-eaters**, **rollers** and **shrikes** are also fond of perching on phone wires and on the branches of thorn trees. Other common birds include cheeky, raucous **mynahs** whose cackles, whoops and whistles are heard everywhere. Circling over fields, along the coast and anywhere where there is rubbish, you may spot white-fronted **brahminy kites** and **vultures** scavenging for food.

Goa's countryside becomes wilder as you head inland towards the Western Ghats (mountain range). In eastern and southern Goa three wildlife reserves have been set aside to protect what is left of the state's virgin forest and wildlife.The **Bondla Wildlife Sanctuary**, not far from Ponda in east central Goa, is the most accessible of these. The **Bhagwan Mahavir Sanctuary**, close to the eastern state border with Karnataka, is perhaps the most spectacular and is dominated by the steep, wooded Western Ghats range. Close to Goa's southern border, the **Cotigao**

◀ *Left: A Slender Loris, which is rather like a lemur, is found widespread in southern India.*

Sanctuary has until recently been the least accessible of the three. All three reserves offer superb birdlife, smaller common mammals including **langur** and **macaque monkeys**, **gaur** (wild cattle) and **antelope** including nilgai, sambar, and chital. The parks also shelter a few **elephant**, **leopard** and even **tiger**, but only the luckiest visitor is likely to spot them even at a distance.

HISTORY IN BRIEF

Known under many different names, Goa has a rather chequered history stretching into the far distant past. Long before the arrival of the Portuguese, the control over Goa's

Ancient Traders

The region was known to the ancient Greeks as **Nelkinda**, and appeared on the charts and accounts of far lands drawn up by the cartographer Ptolemy of Alexandria in the third century bc. Traders from the Arab and Persian cities of the Arabian Gulf, who knew it as **Sindabur**, were long established along the coast by the time the Portuguese arrived.

Tamdi Surla

Tamdi Surla temple is the only major building from the period of the **Kadamba** kings which survives in Goa. Unlike the temples around Ponda it has not been repeatedly restored or modernized. The high quality of its carvings of Brahma, Vishnu, Shiva and Parvati hint at the glories of **Govapuri**, the Kadamba city. This city stood close to the site of Old Goa and which has now completely vanished. Tamdi Surla's layout, its shikara (spire) and many of its details are similar to those of the Chalukyan temples of Maharashtra, and help to date the temple to the 12th or 13th century.

valuable natural harbours was contested by Hindu and Muslim princes. The Portuguese arrived in the 15th century and so Goa became a Portuguese colony, unlike the rest of the sub-continent which formed part of the British Raj. Goa remained a Portuguese enclave until 1961.

Goa's first **Dravidian** people mixed with settlers from the north, firstly from the **Indus Valley**, then with the **Aryan** invaders who began to arrive in India around 1500BC. From around the 3rd century BC, Goa came under the control of a number of would-be empire builders as part of the region then known as the **Konkan**. By the 12th century it had become a distinct realm ruled by the **Hindu Kadamba** dynasty, with its capital, **Govapuri**, on the banks of the Zuari River where the ruins of Goa Velha now stand. Its natural harbours also attracted traders from the Arab world, but very few reminders of this era survive, as later waves of invaders ruthlessly destroyed the palaces and temples of the land they conquered.

The Muslims

Around the end of the 12th century, the Hindu states of northern India had been conquered by **Muslim Turks**, who built an empire which controlled much of northern India with its capital in Delhi. At first, this had little impact on affairs in the south but gradually the Muslim conquerors fell out amongst themselves. In the late 14th century, a fresh wave of **Turkish** invaders led

▼ Below: Fishing boats moored on the Mandovi where the first Portuguese navigators landed.

by the great **Timur** destroyed the Delhi sultanate, making way for a host of small, independent Muslim and Hindu kingdoms.

In the south, the two most important of these were the Muslim **Bahminis**, ruling an empire stretching across what is now Karnataka, and the Hindu **Vijayanagars**. For the next century, they were locked in a struggle for control of southwest India.

The Bahminis first succeeded in ousting the last of Goa's Kadamba rulers some time in the first half of the 14th century, only to lose Goa to the Vijayanagars a quarter of a century later. Wars continued between the two kingdoms throughout the 15th century and in 1470 the Muslim general **Mahmud Gawan** finally drove the Vijayanagars out. The **Bahmini** empire broke up towards the end of the 15th century, and when the first Portuguese caravels sailed into the mouth of the Mandovi, they found near its mouth the thriving main seaport of a Muslim state called **Bijapur**, ruled by **Yusuf Adil Shah**.

▲ *Above: Portuguese Captain-General, Afonso de Albuquerque.*

The Portuguese

During the late 15th and early 16th centuries, the tiny Atlantic nation of Portugal launched an astonishing series of voyages of discovery in the east. The Muslim conquests of Palestine and Byzantium, completed in the mid-15th century, had cut Europe off from the wealth of Asia and Portuguese captains sought a new route around Africa.

In 1488 the navigator **Bartolomeo Dias** rounded the Cape of Good Hope to find himself in the open seas of the Indian Ocean. Ten years later, a fleet commanded by **Vasco da Gama** went even further, reaching Calicut (now Kozhikode) in Kerala. Later expeditions, in 1500 and 1502, strengthened Portugal's hand and the Raja of Cochin allowed Da Gama to build a fortress there in return for his help against the rival Raja of Calicut.

The Empire Builder

Afonso de Albuquerque was the architect of Portugal's overseas empire. Within 10 years of Dias rounding Africa, Afonso had established Portuguese strongholds on the East African coast. By 1510 Goa was his. A year later he conquered Malacca, on the west coast of Malaysia, then sailed on east to seize Macau, in southern China. Fifteen years after his arrival, Portuguese ships had driven the Arabs from the Indian Ocean and the King of Portugal claimed to be 'Lord of the Conquest, Navigation and Commerce of Ethiopia, Arabia, Persia and India'.

The rajas of the Indian coast were eager to become allies of the new arrivals. Portuguese ships and cannon, far superior to those of local rulers, would be a mighty advantage in the never-ending wars with their Muslim neighbours and Hindu rivals. The Portuguese, meanwhile, were delighted to find that the ports of western India could – as they had hoped – give them access to the fantastically lucrative spice trade of India, Ceylon (Sri Lanka) and the East Indies (Indonesia).

In 1510, the greatest of Portugal's commanders, **Afonso de Albuquerque**, arrived with a fresh fleet. With the connivance of the Raja of Vijayanagar and the local Hindus who, in fact, resented Muslim rule, Albuquerque swept into Goa and in 10 months of hard fighting on land and sea drove out the forces of the Adil Shah to raise the Portuguese flag.

With Goa secured, Albuquerque pushed on east, conquering Malacca on the Malaysian peninsula. Later, Portuguese admirals added possessions in the East Indies, Ceylon and Macau, while others consolidated Portuguese control of a chain of territories stretching all the way around Africa. Goa became known as 'Goa Doirada' or '**Golden Goa**' and it was the most important link in this chain. Albuquerque set out to turn Goa into a mirror image of Portugal, importing priests to convert the Goanese to the Catholic faith and encouraging his soldiers and settlers to marry the local women, and found a new nation loyal to Portugal. This racially enlightened policy was maintained throughout the years of Portuguese rule and undoubtedly played a major part in contributing to the easy-going Goa of today.

Portugal's first territories – the central provinces of Ilhas, Bardez, and Salcete – are still known as the **Old Conquests**. Much later, in the 17th and 18th centuries, the Portuguese added the provinces of Bicholim, Sanguem, Ponda, Quepem and Canacona which became known as the **New Conquests**. By the mid-17th century the Portuguese capital, now known as Velha Goa, was one of the marvels of the East, a glittering capital to rival Lisbon and outshine Paris or London.

Holy Orders

Old Goa's churches were founded and controlled by several different **Catholic** orders, all of which followed the Portuguese flag east in search of converts. They set up their headquarters in the colonial capital. The first to reach Goa were the **Franciscans**, who arrived soon after Albuquerque's conquest of the city and built their first convent in 1517. In 1835, a newly liberal Portuguese government ordered the dissolution of the religious orders in Portuguese territories, and many of the buildings of Old Goa were abandoned.

Historical Calendar

973AD Goa first appears in historical records as Gove or Gopakkapattana, capital of the Kadamaba King Shastadeva I.
14th century Muslim expansion into southern India.
1325 Muhammad bin Tughluq Sultan of Delhi. Gopakkapattana sacked by Muslim invaders.
1345–1470 Goa disputed by Kadamba, Bahmini and Vijayanagar kingdoms.
1490 Bahmini empire disintegrates. Goa passes to Yusuf Adil Shah of Bijapur.
1498 Vasco da Gama's fleet arrives in Calicut.
1500–1502 Portuguese expeditions continue to arrive in India.
1510 Afonso de Albuquerque, Portuguese Captain-General, seizes Goa from the Adil Shah.
Late 16th century Portuguese consolidate hold on Goa, expand eastwards.
1795 Portuguese Viceroy moves residence from Velha Goa to Panaji.
1763 Portuguese seize Cabo de Rocha island.
1781 Bicholim conquered by Portuguese.
1782 Portuguese conquer Satari, from native ruler.
1791 King of Sunda cedes Ponda, Sanguem, Quepem and Canacona by treaty.
1799–1813 British occupy Goa to deny it to France.
1818–58 British Raj expands over Indian subcontinent.
1947 British India partitioned into Pakistan and India. Goa remains under Portuguese rule.
1948 Nehru demands Goa's return to India.
1961 Indian forces invade Goa. Portugal surrenders.
1961–87 Goa directly ruled from New Delhi.
1987 Goa achieves statehood.
1998 Completion of Konkan Railway Mumbai-Goa (Vasco) and Ernakulam.
2004 Nonstop express rail service introduced between Goa and Delhi; Goa hosts International Film Festival of India for first time.
2008 More than 460 people killed and injured by Islamic terrorist attacks on hotels in Mumbai.
2014 New international airport terminal inaugurated in Mumbai.
2015 Work scheduled to begin on new international airport in northern Goa (phase 1 to be completed in 2020).

European Rivals

New European rivals were beginning to appear in Indian waters; first the **Dutch**, then the **French** and then lastly the **British**. For the next century Britain, France and their Indian allies battled for control of the subcontinent. By the end of the 18th century Britain had ousted France. With the defeat of the great Indian uprising of 1857–1858 (still sometimes referred to as the Indian Mutiny) the British Raj was supreme from the Himalayas to Cape Comorin and remained so until its partition into independent India and Pakistan in 1947.

▼ Below: The Portuguese colonial legacy includes gracious old-fashioned family homes.

These momentous events largely passed Goa by, though it was occupied by the British between 1799 and 1813. Portugal was unable to keep up its imperial impetus, and its scattered empire languished. 'Golden Goa' went into decline as a succession of plagues rather than wars killed many of its people and in the early 19th century the capital moved to Panjim (now known as Panaji). Portuguese neutrality kept Goa out of both world wars and made Panaji a hotbed of espionage by both Allied and Axis agents during World War II.

MAHATMA MOHANDAS GANDHI

Gandhi was born in 1869, the son of the prime minister of the small state of **Porbandar**. He studied law in London, then worked as a lawyer in South Africa until the age of 46. On his return to India, he became a leader of the independence movement, preaching non-violence. He abandoned European garb for the cotton dhoti and won the title 'Mahatama' (Great Soul) from his followers. He led India to independence in 1947, only to be assassinated the following year by a Hindu fanatic who was outraged by Gandhi's rejection of the caste system.

Union with India

The rest of India achieved independence from Britain in 1947, and the Indian government immediately demanded that Goa too should become part of the newly independent state. The Portuguese government refused, and over the next 14 years relations between the two countries deteriorated until, on 17 December 1961, Prime Minister **Jawaharlal Nehru** ordered Indian forces to invade the Portuguese enclave. Faced with overwhelming force, the Portuguese surrendered without resisting on 19 December, and after four and a half centuries of Portuguese rule, Goa became part of the Republic of India.

Most of the agitation for Goa to be absorbed into India came from **Indian nationalists** outside the province. Within Goa, many of the large Portuguese-speaking Christian minority were less enthusiastic. Under Portuguese rule they controlled most of Goa's trade and industry and the lower ranks of its bureaucracy. They were reluctant to see Goa absorbed into one of the much larger neighbouring states, and they feared that an influx of carpet-baggers would deprive them of their privileged social status.

Happily, **independence** proved mainly beneficial to Goa. The Portuguese were not great believers in overseas investment, and in fact were actively opposed to modernization. At the end of the colonial era Goa still lacked most of the amenities of the 20th century. There were no tarred roads or electricity outside Panaji, no airport, no modern port facilities, and virtually no telephone or telegraph system. There were no public health facilities, the education system was rudimentary, and there was practically no industry or modern farming.

Goa was a somnolent backwater isolated not only from the rest of India but from most of the outside world. Union with India brought substantial planned investment and modernization. This included a road and telecommunications network which now embraces all of Goa's main towns and villages; new bridges to span the state's rivers; a public health, education and welfare system; new farming techniques; better port facilities and the beginnings of an industrial infrastructure.

Jawaharlal Motilal Nehru

Gandhi's successor was very different. A western-influenced aristocrat with the common touch, he was committed to making India a mechanized modern society and to raising living standards. The true architect of modern India, he dominated politics until his death in 1964, founding a political dynasty which dominated Indian politics until the assassination of his grandson, Prime Minister Rajiv Gandhi, by Tamil extremists in 1990.

◀ *Opposite: Mahatma 'Great Soul' Mohandas Gandhi.*
▼ *Below: Hotel Cidade de Goa stands on its own beach close to Panaji.*

The Flag

India's national flag is a tricolour of **orange**, **white** and **green** horizontal stripes. In the centre, a stylized **spinning wheel** is a memento of Gandhi's drive to restore Indian self-sufficiency in place of dependence on western imports. Gandhi made the traditional spinning wheel a symbol of the struggle for independence not only from British rule but from western values which he felt were undermining India's spiritual welfare.

The Latest Invasion

For good or ill, the **tourism** boom has been the biggest factor in changing the face of Goa. Not only Europeans flock to the state in search of fun and relaxation: nine out of ten visitors are from elsewhere in India. Meanwhile, thousands of Indians from less prosperous states migrate to Goa in pursuit of tourist rupees, finding work as market traders, hotel and restaurant staff, drivers and cleaners. Homeless street children from India's cities also ride the trains to Goa to beg from tender-hearted tourists.

Until the 1980s most visitors were budget travellers, but the internationalization of **Dabolim Airport** (originally a navy base) opened the state to mass-market tourism. Foreign visitor numbers grew from fewer than 9000 in 1973 to more than three million arrivals by 2013, an overall increase of 12% on the previous year. Foreign visitor numbers, however, increased by only 4%, with more than two million tourists arriving in the state from within India. Visitor numbers are predicted to reach six million by 2016.

Work on a new airport at Mopa in northern Goa, originally due for completion in 2014, had not yet begun by 2015. The project has been delayed by opposition from major hotel interests in southern Goa, who fear it will siphon off their business to the north. However, the government now plans to run the new airport in tandem with Goa's existing airport at Dabolim to bring increased tourism to north and south Goa.

A Democratic Giant

With more than 850 million people, India is by far the world's largest democracy. Even though Indian politics are frequently marred by communal violence – which Goa has escaped – the country has avoided lurching into right- or left-wing extremism. In any case, conventional political labels are largely meaningless in the Indian context.

GOVERNMENT AND ECONOMY

Since 1987 Goa has been a fully fledged state of the Republic of India, electing its own state assembly which has control over the police, the education system, agriculture and industrial matters. Goa also elects its own members of the two houses of the national parliament in New Delhi.

India's governmental system is parliamentary, with a 500-member lower house called the **Lok Sabha** (House of the People) and a 250-member upper house called the **Rajya Sabha** (Council of States). The two houses, together with the state assemblies, elect a figurehead president but the reins of power are in the hands of the prime minister.

Economic Development

The abject poverty which strikes any visitor masks the fact that after more than 20 years of precocious economic growth the number of Indians living in poverty has fallen from around 50% to under one in three. More than 75% now own a mobile phone, and there has been an eightfold increase in car ownership. Much of this is down to a quarter-century of policy changes that opened up the country's centrally-planned, protectionist economy to foreign imports and competition. Not all the results have been beneficial. Millions of Indians have no permanent work and lack the benefits that go with steady employment, such as pensions and medical insurance. In Mumbai, many survive by begging or scavenging. For urban slum dwellers and rural villagers alike, life is very insecure.

▼ *Below: Fishing trawlers crowd the harbour at Panaji. Much of their catch is exported.*

Industry and Agriculture

Despite all this, most Indians make their living from the land, as they always have. This is especially true in Goa, which has very little industry apart from the extensive open-cast mining operations around Bicholim, in central Goa. The state produces around 30% of India's iron ore, most of it exported through the port of Mormugao at the mouth of the Zuari. Tourism is poised to become an even more important foreign currency earner. **Fishing** is quickly being industrialized, and canned sardines and frozen shellfish have become important export items. This probably means that Goa's small-boat fishermen are doomed and the days of cheap prawns and lobster are numbered.

Coconuts, cashews and rice are Goa's staple **crops**. Most of Goa's rice is grown in the fertile, low-lying land of the Old Conquests, with planting occurring both during the monsoon and in the dry winter season. Coconuts and cashews are very important, with almost half of the state's cultivated land devoted to one or the other.

▼ *Below: Palm trees line the coast at Palolem.*

THE PEOPLE

With a population of 1.5 million (2011 estimate), Goa is a drop in India's ever-increasing ocean of almost 1.3 billion people (2011 estimate). As a result, articulate Goanese often feel that their state has little chance of making itself heard in New Delhi or getting positive results from the Government of India – a view often put forward stridently in the local press.

Though **Portuguese** is no longer very widely spoken, the influence of four centuries of Portuguese colonial rule is still strong, and Portuguese surnames like Mascarenhas or D'Souza are common amongst the state's older Christian familes and in the business, political and academic elite.

Just over 30% of Goa's people are Christians, most of them **Roman Catholics**, and the state is dotted with Christian churches. In general, most of Goa's Christians are found in Panaji and along the coast, which historically is the area of the greatest Portuguese influence. Here, there seem to be churches at every turn, most of them built on the site of earlier temples and mosques razed by the Portuguese. Despite the high profile of the Christian community, proportionally by far the biggest of any Indian state, most of Goa's people are **Hindus**. They predominate in the inland rural communities, and the visitor is far more likely to spot the characteristically colourful Hindu temples in locations well away from the coast. Ethnic and religious frictions are quite rare – perhaps because the two main communities are geographically separate.

Visitors arriving in Goa from other parts of India are often pleasantly surprised by the rather reserved friendliness of most Goans. There is very little of the frenzied hassle and hard sell which plagues the tourist circuit of northern India. Local people, however, are divided in their feelings about the flood of **tourism** which is now pouring into their once-quiet backwater. The first visitors to arrive in numbers were the hippies of the 1960s, who found in Goa a tranquil resting place after the rigours of overland travel. Many of Goa's less-accessible beaches are still favoured by alternative

Caste System

There are many sub-castes, but Hinduism is mainly dominated by four castes: **Brahmins**, or priests; **Kshatriyas**, or warriors and rulers; **Vaisyas** or merchants and farmers; and **Sudras** or artisans and manual workers. The hierarchy is rigid, with no way of changing caste. Outside the caste system are the widely oppressed people called 'untouchables' – because their touch, or even their shadow, is believed to defile upper-caste people. Gandhi sought to improve their position, calling them the '**Harijans**' (Children of God).

▶ *Right: Mumbai, India's film capital, churns out thousands of blockbusters every year.*

travellers, whose sex, drugs and rock and roll lifestyle is disliked by local conservatives – and by tourism developers who fear the hippies deter the more lucrative package holiday-makers.

Meanwhile, runaway tourism development has also been accused by local and international pressure groups of driving villagers off their land, destroying the livelihood of local fisherfolk and polluting beaches and the sea. The debate continues, but the tourism boom shows no signs of slackening.

Language

India's official language is **Hindi**, the mother tongue of around half the country's people, but in a country of so many different races and ethnic groups there are literally hundreds of regional languages and dialects.

Hindi is most widely spoken in northern India, and central

Language

The Portuguese conquerors tried to stamp out **Konkani**, the most widely spoken language in Goa, and force the populace to speak Portuguese. The attempt failed and so today hardly any Goans can speak Portuguese. English is still a vital means of communication in India, and it is the language in which children are taught at school. There are many different dialects in Goa: Hindi is spoken in the North whilst Tamil, Kannada, Telugu and Malayalam are spoken in the South.

government efforts to make it the sole national language of government and education have become a hot political issue down south.

Southern states have stubbornly resisted the sidelining of their own more widely used languages, which are descended from the **Dravidian** tongue of the first dwellers in the region. The most widespread of these is **Tamil**, spoken in the south-east. To the south and east of Goa, the main languages are **Kannada**, **Telugu** and **Malayalam**.

All over India, but especially in the south, **English** is a vital second language and is universally spoken in government, business circles and the tourism industry.

India has scores of English-language newspapers, including the country's most influential, *The Times of India*. In conversation with each other, Indians often switch with ease from English into Hindi or other regional languages. English-language newspaper stories and everyday speech are spiced with Hindi expressions which can make conversation hard to follow.

Goa has one of the highest literacy rates in India (almost 90%) and English is widely spoken. Almost everyone you are likely to meet in shops, hotels, and restaurants will speak enough English for you to get by. Taxi drivers usually speak some English, and railway personnel are usually quite fluent. This is true also in the main towns and beach resorts of neighbouring Kerala and Karnataka, where many people speak basic English.

Out in the countryside, though, it's a different story. In northern Goa, people may speak **Marathi**, the language of the neighbouring Maharashtra state. Goa's own language, **Konkani**, has been recognized as an independent tongue since 1976 and is widely spoken.

Portuguese, on the other hand, has died out quite rapidly since 1961, and survives mainly in the kitchen and on restaurant menus, where peculiarly Goan-Portuguese dishes have survived the demise of the Portuguese empire.

In the next-door state of Karnataka, which sees far fewer foreign tourists, English is not widely spoken outside the

Indian Scripts

Most Indian languages have their own script. Few visitors will have time to master the complicated character systems used; however, English signage is virtually universal throughout Goa, Mumbai and southern India, so the visitor will encounter few problems.

Indian Epics

India's two greatest epics are the Ramayana and the Mahabharata. **Ramayana** tells the story of an eons-long war between Rama and his allies and Ravana, the demon-king of Lanka. In the **Mahabharata** story, five good brothers, with the help of Krishna, battle against 100 evil cousins and their demon helpers. Together with the Bhagavad Gita (the greatest of the Hindu sacred texts), and the Vedas, Upanishads and Puranas, these form the basis of the Hindu faith and all Hindu poetry.

major cities of Mysore and Bengaluru. The most widely used language is **Kannada**. In Kerala, to the south, English is much more widely spoken. A series of Marxist state governments committed to education have given the state the highest literacy rate in India (around 93%, almost double the national average) and the nation's highest life expectancy .

Malayalam, Kerala's main language, is closely related to Tamil, the largest language group in southern India and the main language of Tamil Nadu state, which occupies India's southwest tip.

Religion

India's history stretches back 4000 years, and each wave of people migrating into the subcontinent has brought a new faith or added to an existing one. Most Indians follow the **Hindu** faith, but there are sizable minorities of other nationalities, most notably **Muslims** (around 80 million) and **Sikhs** (around 15 million) with smaller minorities of **Buddhists** (around five million) and **Jains** (around three million).

Goa does not reflect the national picture. Most of its people (more than 60%) are Hindu, but Christians, who are a tiny minority in most other Indian states, are the second largest group (almost 40%). Muslims make up only 3% of the population. As a result, Goa has escaped the occasional clashes between Hindus and Muslims, Hindus and Sikhs, or between all three, which mar Indian politics.

Hinduism

Hinduism is the oldest and most complex faith in the world. India's first civilization, in the Indus Valley, held early Hindu beliefs. The Aryan invaders who started to arrive around 1500BC added new gods to the already extensive pantheon and created the complex caste system which survives more or less intact today.

▲ *Above: Hindu temples, like this one at Margao, are usually brightly painted and scented with aromatic essences.*
◀ *Opposite: Hindu holy men called* sadhus *perform seemingly miraculous feats at traditional festivals.*

With its dozens of deities, many of whom have several different personalities, Hinduism can be baffling to the outsider. In a sense, however, each Hindu god can be seen as just one aspect of a single supreme being.

There are three major deities: Brahma, the creator; Vishnu, the preserver; and Shiva, who represents destruction and rebirth. All-seeing **Brahma**, the most distant of the gods, is shown with four faces, often accompanied by his consort **Sarasvati**, the goddess of wisdom, riding a white swan. **Shiva** is often represented by the stone lingam, and is depicted riding a bull and bearing a trident. One of his aspects is **Nataraja**, the dancer who created the world. His consort, **Parvati**, is the great beauty of the Hindu pantheon. She has two less charming sides to her nature: **Kali**, the death-goddess, with her girdle of human skulls, and **Durga**, the goddess of destruction, multi-limbed, armed and mounted on a tiger.

Vishnu is perhaps the most human of the gods, appearing on Earth in a series of incarnations symbolizing the nine ages of the Earth. Vishnu rides the mighty Garuda bird and his consort is **Lakshmi**, goddess of wealth and prosperity. In his first six incarnations he appeared as a wild boar or a manticore (half-man, half-lion). In his seventh he appeared as **King Rama**, leader of mankind and the gods against the demons in Hinduism's most accessible epic, the Ramayana. In his eighth, he came as the playful **Krishna**, brought up by shepherds and famed for his romps with pretty shepherd-esses. In paintings and temple carvings he is coloured blue and plays the flute.

Hindu Temples

A typical Hindu temple is a riot of colour, with a many-tiered spire encrusted with brilliantly painted gods, demons, and mythical creatures. Inside, incense burns in front of garlanded images or phallic Shiva lingams. Offerings of rice are often made, and you will probably be asked to contribute a small sum to the upkeep of the temple. Old and disabled people often beg out-side temples. should you wish to give, have a pocketful of small change ready.

Banned

Ironically, Mumbai-born British author **Salman Rushdie**'s controversial novel *The Satanic Verses* is banned in his native city because certain verses offend devout Muslims. In view of this, indian politicians support the ban as they are reluctant to risk losing the votes of the almost 80 million-strong Muslim community.

Hinduism also has a large supporting cast of lesser deities, like Krishna's faithful sidekick **Hanuman**, the monkey god, and **Ganesha**, the elephant-headed son of Shiva and Parvati and god of wisdom and wealth; part of the religion's age-old appeal is the existence of a god to turn to in every aspect of everyday life, from bringing up children to catching fish, planting rice or investing money. Also appealing is the notion of rebirth: things may not be so great as a poor rice farmer in this life, but there is always the possibility of re-incarnation as a wealthy man in the next life, or the one after that.

Christianity

Vasco da Gama told the Indians of the Malabar coast (now Kerala) that he had come seeking 'Christians and spices'. He found both, for southern India is the site of the world's oldest Christian community, founded by **St Thomas the Apostle** in AD52 and boosted by the arrival of Christian merchants from the Levant towards the end of the 2nd century AD.

The **Portuguese** imposed Christianity on Goa by the sword and by conversion. Their assault on Islam was ruthless. Goa's Muslim inhabitants were slaughtered or driven into exile and their mosques were razed. Their approach to the Hindus was less violent. Many converts came from the lower castes or the

▼ *Below: Statue of Jesus facing the Se Cathedral, Old Goa.*

▲ *Above: Earthenware pots are in everyday use in the kitchens of India.*

Dalit community. Catholicism offered them a way out of the rigid caste system, or so it seemed, while its pantheon of the Holy Trinity, the Virgin Mary, and a colourful array of saints and apostles must have seemed not too different from the familiar Hindu pantheon. The Portuguese did, however, destroy Hindu temples in the Old Conquests. By the 18th century they had become less destructive, and Goa's oldest temples are located in the New Conquest provinces which spent less time under Portugal.

The Arts

The performing arts in India today are part of a continuous artistic tradition stretching back into antiquity. From the earliest times, Indian artists have been masters of the plastic arts, producing superbly graceful and dignified stone images of gods, kings and dancers. Ancient temples and holy caves are decorated with fluid frescoes, often depicting scenes from the great Hindu epics, the **Ramayana** and the **Mahabharata**. Modern artists too are still strongly influenced by the colours, the strong lines, and above all the narrative tradition embodied in traditional Hindu art, in which every picture tells a story, with more than 3000 years of complex myths and legends to draw on.

Music and **dance** are equally closely involved with Hindu beliefs. There are dances from every part of India, and for every occasion. Male and female dancers rarely if ever appear together, and in many dances, the female roles are performed by men. Many dances tell the stories of the gods and their battles with demons or encounters with mortals. Rama's prowess in the Ramayana or Krishna's flirtations with mortal maidens are popular themes of traditional dance.

▶ *Right: Kathakali dancers in Kochi prepare for a performance by applying layers of their vividly coloured make-up.*

Teatri is another Goan tradition – a vaudeville-style life show with musicians and comic singers who often satirize local politicians or hotels.

India's **movie** industry is one of the world's biggest, with a huge and voracious audience awaiting each new Hindi epic. Stars have godlike status, and several actors – male and female – have gone on to become leading politicians at both state and national level, having been swept to power by the votes of millions of adoring cinema fans.

Most Indian films are made in the giant studios of Mumbai, often nicknamed 'Bollywood'. Stars and directors work hard, often filming several movies simultaneou sly, and the output is phenomenal.

The plots are simple and melodramatic, usually with a romantic male and female lead, an obvious villain, and a stock supporting cast. Happy endings are the norm, but it's not unusual for the heroine to die tragically in the last reel. The entire cast breaks into song and dance at every opportunity, even in all-action productions, and since most Hindi epics run to about three hours, watching one can be an emotionally draining experience.

Goa first hosted the International Film Festival of India in April 2004 and the event now seems to have become an annual fixture, attracting film-makers from Mumbai and

WINES

Imported wines, found only in upmarket hotels, are usually overpriced and of indifferent quality. Grapes are grown on the higher, cooler country of the **Karnataka** plateau around Hyderabad, which has an almost Californian climate. You may find locally made wines in some restaurants. In general, Indian white wines (if served very cold) are better than the reds. Indian sparkling wines have also improved enormously in recent years, and labels such as **Marquise de Pompadour** and **Ivy Brut** are widely available in Mumbai and Goa.

producers, writers, directors and critics from all over the world (*see* www.iffigoa.org for future dates).

Food and Drink

Goa has some of the finest food in India, and its cuisine is less intimidating to inexperienced western palates than that of some other Indian states.

Seafood, including all sorts of fish and prawns, figure high on the menu, though the delicious tiger prawns and langouste which used to be such an affordable delight should be on the endangered list – they command high prices abroad and most of the catch is frozen for export. The commonest **fish** is the *bangra*, similar to a large sardine, which may be served freshly grilled, simmered in a spicy tomato sauce, or in many other ways. Crispy fried pomfret, a small sea-fish, is a favourite snack.

Pork, which is found nowhere else in India – both Hindus and Muslims consider the pig an unclean animal – is eaten with relish by the Christian Goans, usually generously flavoured with garlic. Other meats on the menu include mutton and sometimes goat. More westernized tourist restaurants will also serve steaks or hamburgers.

Like every Indian region, Goa has its own special **curry** dishes. The Goan version of vindaloo, called *vindalhao*, features pork simmered in garlic, vinegar and chillies. Many dishes are served *reichado*, stuffed with chillies and other spices. *Cabidel* is a favourite spicy pork stew, and *xacati*, chicken served with coconut-flavoured rice, is another spicy dish.

Everything comes with rice – though in the more tourist-oriented restaurants french fries are usually offered as an option – and main dishes are usually accompanied by the flapjack-like *chapatis* or flat nan bread, originating in northern India but now found everywhere.

If you're travelling off the tourist trail, one of the best bets throughout India is to order a *thali*, which is a vegetarian set meal featuring various kinds of *dal* (lentil stew), pickles, and curds.

Spirits and Beers

Goa's own tipple, ***feni***, is made from the fermented sap of the coconut palm or from the fermented juice of the cashew nut. A clear, fiery spirit, it is an acquired taste. which few visitors in fact find appealing. More palatable are the various Indian rums (all gold or dark) and whiskies. The best are blends of Scotch malt with local spirit. Beers include the excellent **Kingfisher**, in large 750ml bottles, and a variety of expensive imports.

2
Mumbai: Gateway to Goa

The huge, sprawling Mumbai Metropolitan area is home to more than 22 million people. This is India in miniature, with all its extremes of wealth, poverty, colour, sound and smells. '[Mumbai] is a crowd,' writes Naipaul. 'Such a torrent of people swept across the road, in such a bouncing froth of light-coloured lightweight clothes, it seemed that some kind of invisible sluice-gate had been opened, and that if it wasn't closed again the flow of road-crossers would spread everywhere, and the beaten-up red buses and yellow-and-black taxis would be quite becalmed, each at the centre of a human eddy.'

With its blocks of grimy apartment buildings and offices, brightened by the garishly painted signboards of shops and businesses, Mumbai is not a pretty city, but it vibrates with the urban urgency of millions of people in motion, day or night.

Previously called Bombay and recently redubbed **Mumbai** – its original Hindi name – by the Hindi fundamentalist government of Maharashtra state, it is cosmopolitan in the truest sense of the word and is home to people from all over India and indeed all over the world. Sheer weight of numbers, and the head-spinning contrasts of grimy bazaars and elegant shops, squalid slums and five-star hotels, temples, mosques and brand new office blocks, can overwhelm the visitor.

Mumbai grew up on a group of marshy islets off the coast of **Gujarat**. Given to Portugal in 1534 by the Sultan of Gujarat, it passed to Britain as the dowry of the Portuguese princess Catherine de Braganza, wife of Charles II, and in 1668 was leased

Don't Miss

*** **Chhatrapati Shivaji Vastu Sanghralaya:** one of the finest collections of Indian art in the world in a splendid historic building.
*** **Elephanta Caves:** magnificent carvings and frescoes in temples carved into the rock.
** **Gateway of India:** splendid stone arch and relic of the heyday of the British Raj.

◀ *Opposite: The Gateway of India, on Mumbai's seafront, is a picturesque relic of the British Raj.*

to the British East India Company. Under British rule it grew to become the biggest seaport on the west coast of India. The opening of the **Suez Canal** in 1869 gave the already thriving city a further economic boost. Mumbai had the greater advantage over Calcutta as it was closer to the European markets. On independence, it became the state capital of **Maharashtra**.

Over the centuries, Mumbai's islands have merged into one large, roughly triangular island, about 60km (37½ miles) long, broadest at its northern end, and tapering to a narrow southern tip, the **Colaba Causeway**. The heart of the city is built on the northern end of this narrow promontory, with the harbour to the east. **Marine Drive** (Netaji Subhash Road), the main city esplanade, sweeps northwest along the shore of Back Bay on the west side of the island. Malabar Point shelters Back Bay from the open sea to the west and is crowned by **Malabar Hill**, the city's most expensive residential district. Running parallel to Marine Drive, **Mahatma Gandhi Road** is the location of most of Mumbai's historic public buildings and cuts through the heart of the city. This part of Mumbai clearly shows its colonial heritage, with a collection of grand Georgian and Victorian Gothic buildings bequeathed by the British and still in use. Among the most imposing are the University, easy to find with its 80m (262ft) clock-tower overlooking KB Patil Marg, and the nearby High Court Building, built in 1878. Older buildings on **Horniman Circle** include the city's original Town Hall, opened in 1833, and the even older Customs House dating from 1720.

To the south of the city centre, the Colaba Causeway area is a mix of cheap accommodation and restaurants, shops and market stalls stretching south to the tip of the island.

◀ *Left: A variety of herbs and spices on sale at a street market.*

Boom Town

Mumbai, now a sprawling metropolis, is one of India's newer cities. Until the arrival of the **Portuguese** and later of the **British East India Company** it was no more than a group of swampy islands. Until the mid-19th century it was less important to the British than their bases at Madras and Calcutta, but by the 1850s it had become a boom town and has never looked back, becoming India's most important financial and commercial centre. Most of its population are Hindu, with sizable Muslim, Christian, Jain and Parsi minorities.

Sightseeing Tips

Though Mumbai is India's biggest city it has relatively few major sights, and one day is sufficient to take in its high points. Guided tours tend to pack in a number of less interesting sights, leaving little time to enjoy the more rewarding attractions. Hiring a car with a driver for a morning or afternoon will enable you to move at a more leisurely pace.

Zoroastrians

The Zoroastrians or Parsis of Mumbai are among the last communities of a religion which once had believers throughout western Asia and the Mediterranean. Founded by the prophet *Zarathustra* (Zoroaster) in ancient Persia around the 7th century BC, Zoroastrianism revolves around belief in a single benevolent god, *Ahura Mazda*, in perpetual conflict with the evil spirit Ahriman.

MARINE DRIVE (NETAJI SUBHASH ROAD)

Mumbai's long crescent esplanade stretches from **Nariman Point** at its southeast end to **Malabar Point**, on the opposite side of **Back Bay**. The best way to see the city's main sites is either to book a taxi through your hotel for the day or, more cheaply, to take the half-day guided tour operated by the Maharashtra Tourist Development Corporation. **Flora Fountain** (Hutatma Chowk), at the south end of **Mahatma Gandhi Road**, is the focal point of the downtown business district and the starting point for most guided or independent explorations of the city. Around it are substantial 19th-century buildings evocative of the last days of the Raj. The most impressive is the Gothic Victoria Terminus, India's largest railway station. With its cathedral-like spires, turrets and arched windows it typifies the grandiose architecture of the British in India.

At its northern end, above the city's busy, colourful and grubby Chowpatty Beach, Marine Drive becomes Walkeshwar Road, running down the inner side of Malabar Point. At the southern end of this road, the **Jain Temple** is an unmistakable landmark, its onion-like spire glittering with thousands of mirror mosaic tiles and its walls covered with elaborate carvings.

Taraporewala Aquarium ★★

Midway along Marine Drive, you'll come across this fascinating aquarium, the largest in India, with displays of both freshwater and saltwater specimens. The emphasis here is on large sea-creatures rather than pretty ones. Sharks, rays, and marine turtles can all be seen. Open 11:00–20:00 Tuesday–Saturday, 10:00–20:00 Sunday.

Mani Bhavan Gandhi Sanghralaya ★★★

The home of **Mahatma Gandhi** between 1917 and 1934 is kept as a shrine to his memory, with his simple *charpoy* (pallet-bed), stick and sandals, and the spinning wheel which Gandhi made into a symbol for India. The telephone by the bed was the Mahatma's sole concession to modern technology. In addition to the plain room in which he worked and lived, there

◀ *Left: Modern tower blocks mingle with old-fashioned buildings along Mumbai's waterfront esplanade.*

is an extensive library of texts by and about the makers of Indian independence, and there is also a small theatre in which films about Gandhi, his political struggles and his ideals are shown. 19 Laburnum Road. Open 09:30–18:00 daily. www.gandhi-manibhavan.org

Hanging Gardens (Ferozeshah Mehta Gardens) ★

Crowning Malabar Hill, the Hanging Gardens climb in tiers above Mumbai's water reservoirs. In most Indian cities, public green spaces are given exaggerated reverence and are often less exciting to the European than to the local eye. This garden is no exception. The complicated topiary which adorns these gardens is lovely, however, and well worth a look. The hedges and bushes have been cleverly trimmed into the shapes of elephants, tigers, and other beasts. In addition to this, you'll have a wonderful view of Back Bay and the city from the park.

Hidden away behind a nearby wall are the **Towers of Silence**, where Mumbai's Parsi community leaves its dead to be eaten by carrion birds. The site is closed to non-Parsis.

Mumbai Beaches

Juhu, 20km (12½ miles) north of central Mumbai and close to Santa Cruz airport, is Mumbai's beach suburb, with a number of large hotels. It gets crowded at weekends, and the sand is far from pristine and the water is polluted.

Marve, on the same coast but a further 20km (12½ miles) north, is less built-up. Take note: Mumbai's beaches are unsafe for swimmers during the monsoon season.

Dabba Lunches

Mumbai has more than 2000 *dabbawallas* – members of a select guild of lunch porters who every day collect more than 100,000 home-made packed lunches from the homes of Mumbai's office workers and deliver them across the sprawling city. Most of the *dabbawallas* are illiterate, but an arcane coding system of coloured symbols guides each meal to the right office desk. Each *dabbawalla* carries up to 40 of the metal pails called 'tiffin tins' on a long, narrow wooden tray, racing on foot through the crowds and traffic. It is claimed that fewer than 20 tins go missing on an average day.

FORT AREA AND COLABA

The oldest part of Mumbai, south of Mahatma Gandhi Road, Churchgate and Victoria railway station, is still called the Fort Area though there is no longer any trace of the original Portuguese and British fortifications.

Chhatrapati Shivaji Vastu Sanghralaya ★★★

Allow at least three hours to view this splendid museum, which has one of the finest collections of Indian art in the world and is an architectural gem in itself. Built in 1905 to mark the visit of the Prince of Wales (later King George V), the museum is in the Indo-Saracenic style, an elegant British pastiche of the architecture of the medieval Mughals. For those who have limited time the key gallery on the ground floor provides an overview of more than 4000 years of Indian art, from clay figurines of the earliest Indus Valley civilization to delightful paintings from the 17th-century heyday of the Mughal Empire. If you have plenty of time, you can browse through galleries of statues, secular and temple art, jewellery, archaeological finds, silver and jade from all over the subcontinent.

If the wildlife reserves of Goa or Kerala are in your schedule, take a look at the museum's natural history section. Open 10:15–18:00 daily, www.csmvs.in

Jehangir Art Gallery ★★★

In the landscaped grounds of the Chhatrapati Shivaji Vastu Sanghralaya, the Jehangir Art Gallery houses India's biggest modern art collection, with up to four exhibitions by contemporary Indian painters. The museum is worth a visit mainly for the contrast between old and new artists, but few of the moderns can really compare with the works of the older masters. Open 10:00–17:30, Tuesday–Sunday, www.jehangirartgallery.com

Gateway of India ★★★

King George V made his imperial entry into India in 1911 through a temporary structure where this splendid stone arch was erected in 1923. Designed by George Willet, architect of the Chhatrapati Shivaji Vastu Sanghralaya, the 26m (79ft) gateway has four arches and is another triumph of British-Indian pomp. The statue next to it is of **Shivaji**, the great 16th-century leader of the warlike Maratha people of Maharashtra, who successfully resisted conquest by the Mughals.

ELEPHANTA ISLAND

Elephanta Island, the only one of the original islands to have escaped being absorbed into the city sprawl, is about an hour away by boat from the landing stages beside the Gateway of India. The trip itself is a welcome escape from the heat, grime and bustle of downtown Mumbai and the island's main attraction, the **Elephanta Caves**, is well worth the journey.

The four temples cut into the rock of the island date from the mid-5th to the mid-8th century ad. The main cave, which is reached by 125 shallow steps, is finely decorated to a height of almost 8m (25ft) with intricate friezework and powerful, fluid frescoes of Shiva in his creative and destructive aspects. Sadly, many of these were damaged by the blasphemous Portuguese, who set up a gun battery on the island and used the temple decorations as targets.

◀ *Left: Rock temples on Elephanta Island, an hour away from Mumbai, date from as early as the 5th century.*

Jains

Jainism is among India's smaller religions, with fewer than four million adherents. Like Buddhists, Jains are pacifists, adhering to the principle of ***ahimsa*** – respect for all forms of life and refusing to harm even insects. The sect was founded about 2500 years ago by the Jain teacher, Mahavira.

Mumbai Slums

Millions of Mumbaikars live in slums such as Annawadi and Dharavi, literally in the shadow of the city's gleaming new office and apartment towers. The real estate potential of these neighbourhoods has not gone unnoticed, and the state government is reportedly planning to 'redevelop' **Dharavi** - home to more than 1 million - at a cost of some US$2.4 billion. What will become of those who live there is uncertain.

MUMBAI AT A GLANCE

Best Times to Visit

Some might argue that there is no good time to visit Mumbai. The city is hot all year round, but the 'coolest' months are from **Dec–Mar**, when rainfall is minimal and the maximum day-time temperatures are around 30°C (86°F). Avoid the hot, dry months of Apr and May, and the monsoon months of Jun to mid-Oct. Rainfall is the heaviest in Jun and Jul.

Getting There

Mumbai's Shivaji Chhatrapati Shivaji Airport (tel: 022 6685 0222, www.csia.in) has two domestic terminals (T1A and T1B). A new international terminal, T2, opened in 2014. The domestic and international terminals are 5km apart and are connected by free shuttle buses which run every 20–30 min. Journey time to the city centre is 60–90 min; between terminals, 30 min. A prepaid taxi service is available from both airports. Mumbai has two long-distance railway stations. Beware of confusion: Central Trains go not from the Central Station but from the Chhatrapati Shivaji Station (formerly Victoria Station), close to the Fort area, which handles trains to Karnataka, Maharashtra and onward connections to Goa, as well as services to Madhya Pradesh, Uttar Pradesh, Haryana and Rajasthan. Central Station, north of the city centre, takes care of Western Railway services to Agra, New Delhi, Rajasthan and Gujarat. There are no ferries between Mumbai and Goa but there were proposals to relaunch a **ferry route** in 2015.

Getting Around

Self-drive **car rental** is available, but not advisable. Cars with a driver can be rented from major hotels, tour and travel agencies. **Taxis** are good value for money. Virtually all are Indian-built Ambassadors and not air conditioned. All are metered, though late at night, drivers are reluctant to switch the meter on and you'll have to haggle. **Auto-rickshaws** are all over India. Three-wheeled scooters with a canopy and bench seat behind the driver, are noisy, shaky and open to dust and exhaust fumes, but are cheaper and more plentiful than taxis. They're not metered, and fares must be agreed at the start of your journey. Drivers rarely speak English well and perceive foreigners as soft targets for jacked-up fares. Bargain hard. Mumbai has an extensive **bus** network, with London-style double-decker buses. Fares are cheap, but avoid the morning and evening rush hours. Buses are not air conditioned. A suburban electric **rail** network connects central Mumbai with its suburbs. The line between Churchgate and Central railway stations takes you through the city centre, with intermediary stops.

Where to Stay

Mumbai's better hotels cluster around **Nariman Point**, at the south end of **Marine Parade**, overlooking **Back Bay**.

Luxury

Taj Mahal Palace and Tower, Apollo Bunder, Mumbai 400 001, tel: 022 6665 3366, www.tajhotels.com Best and grandest hotel in Mumbai with superb service, facilities and choice of restaurants. Excellent location next to Gateway of India. Private yacht available.

The Oberoi, Nariman Point, Mumbai 400 021, tel: 022 6632 5757, www.oberoihotels.com Excellent hotel; luxury facilities in Mumbai's finest location.

Grand Hyatt Mumbai, Western Express Highway, tel: 022 6676 1234, www.mumbai.grand.hyatt.com Excellent modern five-star; 20 min from international airport terminal (T2), 10 min from domestic. Wide range of business and leisure facilities, and restaurants.

The Leela Kempinski, Sahar, Andheri, Mumbai 400 059, tel: 022 5691 1234, www.theleela.com The best hotel near the airport terminals.

Mid-range

Ramada Plaza Palm Grove, Juhu Beach, Juhu, Mumbai 400 049, tel: 022 2611 2323, www.ramadaplaza-juhu.com New member of US chain, with a lovely view of Mumbai's up-market suburban beach.

Abode, 1st Floor, Lansdowne House Building, MB Marg, Apollo Bunder, tel 8080 23 40 66, www.abodeboutiquehotels.com Trendy boutique hotel in the heart of Colaba.

Gordon House Hotel, 5 Battery

Street, Apollo Bunder, Mumbai 400 039, tel: 022 2289 4400, www.ghhotel.com Mumbai's first (and so far only) boutique hotel has 29 stylish rooms. Close to Gateway of India.
Waterstones Hotel, International Airport Approach Rd, Sahard Road, tel: 022 409 06633, www.waterstoneshotel.com This boutique hotel is 1.22km from the international airport and 5km from the domestic airport, ideal for an overnight stop between flights or when leaving early or arriving late.

Budget

Galaxy Residency, Anderi-Gahtkopar Link Road, East Mumbai, tel: 022 2511 2814, www.hotelgalaxiresidencyindia.in Modern, businesslike hotel with facilities including room service, WiFi and air con. Free airport transfers.

Where to Eat

Luxury

Mumbai's top restaurants are in major hotels and offer everything from vegetarian Indian cuisine to Chinese, Middle Eastern, Japanese, Thai, Asia-Pacific fusion and Western/international dishes.
Wasabi by Morimoto, Taj Mahal Palace, ext. 3202. Seafood and vegetarian dishes, tempura and sashimi by famed Japanese chef.
Masala Kraft, Taj Mahal Palace, ext. 3278. Modern Indian cooking with a light touch. Excellent wine list.
The China House, Grand Hyatt Mumbai. Newest of the city's upscale Chinese eating places; modern Asian-fusion dishes.
Aer, Four Seasons Hotel, 114 E, Moses Road, Worli, Mumbai, tel: 022 2481 8000 Fantastic views of the city at night from this glitzy rooftop 34 floors up.

Mid-range

Papa Pancho, Gasper Enclave, St John's Road, Pali Hill, tel: 022 3015 1269. Authentic Punjabi cooking, such as chicken *khada masala*, *dal makhani* and *dhaba* mutton.
Cafe Mondegar, Metro House, 5A Shahid Bhagat Singh Road, tel: 022 2202 0591 Lively bar-restaurant with Indian and Western pub food and cold beer.

Shopping

Mumbai is a retail paradise with wholesale prices. The city is one big bazaar: you can buy colonial antiques, Indian spices, silks, gems and designer clothing and accessories. Don't miss 'Fashion Street', a row of stalls on MG Road between Cross Maidan and Azad Maidan, where you can snap up top labels at bargain prices. 'Antiqued' furniture is found in the Chor Bazaar flea market. In all of these, hard haggling is the norm. If bargaining is not your thing, try the government-run Central Cottage Industries Emporium, Shivaji Marg, between Apollo Bunder and Regal, for an assortment of fabrics, furniture, kitchenware, carpets, embroidery, scarves, saris, jewellery, toys and ornaments from all over India. Most shops are open between 10:00 and 19:00, and bazaar stalls from 10:00 until around 21:00.

Tours and Excursions

Maharashtra Tourism Development Corporation, CD Hutments, Madame Cama Road, tel (toll free): 1800 233 5050, www.maharashtratourism.gov.in Operates a wide range of excursions around Mumbai and throughout Maharashtra. Destinations include the Ellora and Ajanta cave temples (*see* p.119–120). Information and bookings for state-run hotels, excursions and bus routes across Maharashtra.

Useful Contacts

India Tourist Development Corporation, 123 Maharishi Karve Road, Mumbai (opposite Churchgate station), tel: 022 291585. Open 08:30–18:00, Mon–Fri; 08:30–13:30, alternate Saturdays. *See* Time Out Mumbai magazine or its web site (www.timeout.com/mumbai) for news of events and the latest restaurant reviews.

MUMBAI	J	F	M	A	M	J	J	A	S	O	N	D
AVERAGE TEMP. °C	24	25	27	28	30	29	27	27	27	28	27	26
AVERAGE TEMP. °F	75	77	81	82	86	84	81	81	81	82	81	79
DAYS OF RAINFALL	1	1	1	1	5	30	30	30	20	10	5	1
RAINFALL mm	2	1	1	3	16	520	710	439	297	88	21	2
RAINFALL in	.1	-	-	.1	.5	20	28	18	12	3.5	.9	.1

3
Panaji and Central Goa

Tiswadi province lies between the **Mandovi** and **Zuari** rivers, tapering towards the narrow western point of Cabo Raj Bhavan. **Panaji** (formerly Panjim), Goa's state capital, lies on the south bank of the broad Mandovi estuary, which broadens to the west into Aguada Bay and the Arabian Sea. Cabo Raj Bhavan separates this bay from the estuary of the Zuari, to the south. Upriver from Panaji lie two river-islands: **Divar**, a genuine island with water on all sides, and **Chorao**, which is in fact a peninsula stretching southwest into the Mandovi from the inland province of Bicholim.

Upriver, too, is **Old Goa**, the long-abandoned Portuguese capital, some 9km (5½ miles) from Panaji. With its ghostly ruined cathedrals on the banks of the Mandovi, this is Goa's most important historic sight and has the biggest concentration of colonial domestic architecture. This colonial capital once stretched all the way between the Mandovi and the Zuari, where the confusingly named present-day village of Goa Velha now stands.

South of the Zuari estuary, the narrow peninsula of **Mormugao** juts west into the Arabian Sea. At the tip of this peninsula is Mormugao harbour, a rather grimy industrial seaport. The airport at nearby Dabolim provides most visitors with their first glimpse of Goa. On the south coast of the peninsula, **Bogmalo** beach is fairly small, handy for the airport, and relatively upmarket. Upriver, the Zuari separates Mormugao from **Ponda** province, where a number of striking Hindu temples cluster around the market town of Ponda.

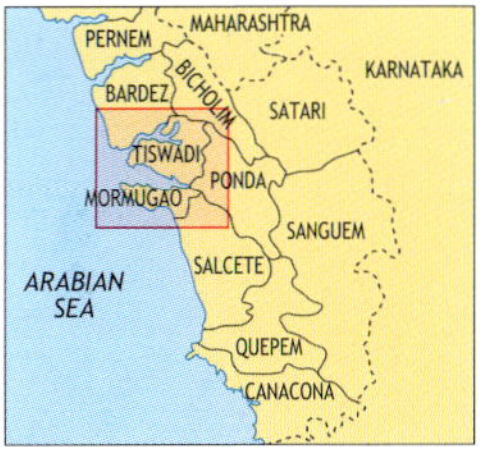

Don't Miss

***** Church of Our Lady of the Immaculate Conception:** this splendid white 17th-century church is Panaji's most striking sight.
***** Old Goa:** remnants of the old Portuguese capital, now abandoned, include mighty churches and triumphal arches.
**** Dona Paula Beach:** the best beach close to Panaji.
**** Bogmalo:** surprisingly uncrowded beach close to Dabolim Airport.

◀ *Opposite: The Church of St Francis is the best preserved in Old Goa.*

PANAJI

Goa's small capital is, surprisingly, relatively free of tourists. It has its own beaches within easy reach, but they are not the best in Goa and most tourists prefer the purpose-built beach resorts of north and south Goa. Though a state capital, Panaji is no metropolis; much of the time it seems to have more in common with a Portuguese market town than with the throbbing urban sprawl of a typical Indian city. You can walk across it in half an hour, and its major sights can be seen during a leisurely morning's shopping and sightseeing. The best time to visit Panaji is first thing in the morning, when the markets are at their liveliest and the sun is not too hot for strolling. The town goes into siesta mode from early afternoon until dusk when things liven up again.

State of Goa

With a population of about 1.3 million and a land area of only 3702km² (1428 sq miles), Goa is India's smallest state. Though churches are to be seen everywhere, less than 40% of the state's population is Christian, while almost 60% is Hindu. Fishing is an important export industry, with canned and frozen fish being exported mainly to the Far East. Rice is the state's largest crop, with coconut and cashew close behind. The state is also a major producer and exporter of iron ore and bauxite from strip mines in the Bicholim area.

Fontainhas District ★★

Ourem Creek, a tributary of the Mandovi, forms central Panaji's eastern boundary. Fontainhas, the old Portuguese quarter immediately west of the creek, is the most pleasant part of town and is made up of three parallel streets which are connected by narrow lanes. Most of the houses here date from the early 19th century, and although the waterfront has lost its charm with the construction of shabby modern buildings, the rest of the district retains its old-fashioned appeal.

Our Lady of the Immaculate Conception ★★★

The dramatic façade of this Catholic Church, with its elaborate white stucco bell-tower, is the most striking sight in Panaji. The church dominates the **Altinho quarter**, which lies between

Fontainhas and the Mandovi waterfront. The first church on the site was built during the earliest years of the Portuguese occupation. It was demolished in 1619 to make way for the present building, which was repeatedly added to and extended throughout the period of Portuguese rule. The most conspicuous addition is the double processional staircase, added in 1871.

Climate

The monsoon season in Goa, between June and mid-September, is the least suitable time for a beach holiday. With less than three hours of sunshine daily in July and August, heavy rain and pounding surf makes swimming dangerous. Many hotels and almost all the state's small beach restaurants close down at this time. However, Goa can be at its most beautiful towards the end of the monsoon season, when fields and coconut groves are a dozen vivid shades of green.

Chapel of St Sebastian ⋆

This small chapel in the Fontainhas district was built in 1888. It houses the crucifix from the headquarters of the **Inquisition** in Old Goa, which was transferred here after the original capital was finally abandoned by the Portuguese during the 19th century.

Government Secretariat (Sultan's Palace) ⋆

The former palace of Yusuf Adil Shah, Sultan of Bijapur and last Muslim ruler of Goa, is a stately arcaded building on the Mandovi waterfront, much altered since the Portuguese took it over. There is no trace of its original fortifications which guarded the approach from the sea.

Municipal Market ⋆

Goa's covered municipal market stretches several blocks inland from the waterfront and spills out into surrounding streets and alleys. Stalls sell a bewildering array of fresh produce, dried fish, household wares, herbs and spices. This is, however, a market for the local people, so not much of the merchandise is aimed specifically at the tourist, but there is plenty to see and buy on the stalls.

BEACHES NEAR PANAJI

Miramar ⋆

Panaji's nearest beach is only 3km (2 miles) west of the city, stretching towards Cabo Raj Bhavan. Its rather grubby sands are a popular escape for local people who use it as an impromptu sports ground and meeting place, but the water is too muddy and the beach too littered to make swimming or sunbathing attractive propositions.

▶ *Right: Goan waters are crystal-clear for much of the year but can be muddy during the rainy season.*

Goa's Muslim Era

Present-day Old Goa was not the first city to be built on this easily defended site with its fine natural harbour. The Kadamba ruler **Jayakeshi I** founded a city called Govapuri near Goa Velha, in the first half of the 11th century. It remained the Kadamba capital until 1343, when it was conquered by the Muslim Sultan, **Jamal ud-Din**. The Kadamba reconquered the city the following year. Some time between 1345 and 1358 it was conquered by the Bahmani Muslims, who in turn lost it to the Hindu king, Vijayanagar. Gopakkapattana survived until 1469, when it was razed to the ground by yet another Bahmani army. The Bahmani conquerors set up their new capital at Ela, where Old Goa now stands, and it was this city that the **Portuguese** took over and expanded. The only surviving trace of the Muslim era is the gate of the Adil Shah's palace.

Dona Paula ★★

This beach on the south side of the Cabo Raj Bhavan headland and 8km (5 miles) from Panaji is a much more attractive stretch of sand. It is overlooked by the landscaped grounds and low buildings of the luxury, Moorish casbah-inspired Hotel Cidade de Goa. Water-skiing and other water sports are available.

OLD GOA

Old Goa, 9km (6 miles) east of Panaji, is Goa's most outstanding sight. On the banks of the **Mandovi** stands a centuries-old complex of mighty churches, monasteries and convents – all that remains of the once-mighty colonial capital which controlled the trade of Portugal's far-flung overseas empire.

Goa's population was reduced by a series of plagues, and the city was gradually abandoned over a period of three centuries. The disused buildings were demolished and the materials used elsewhere. By the early 19th century only the great places of worship were left to mark the site of the city. Even their days were numbered. In 1835 the Portuguese government disestablished the great church orders and most of Goa's religious community scattered, leaving many of the churches to fall into ruin.

The heart of Old Goa is a complex of three adjoining buildings – the **Se Cathedral**, the **Church of St Francis of Assisi**, and the **Archaeological Museum**, formerly the Convent of St Francis. They are set among tidily kept lawns. A statue of the great Portuguese poet and soldier, Luíz Vaz de Camões, stands guard over the approach road.

Se Cathedral ★★★

Commissioned by the Dominican order in 1562, the Se Cathedral was intended to be the greatest church in Portugal's string of Asian colonies. It was not completed until the mid-17th century. Only one of the twin towers survives. The grandiose interior is barrel-vaulted and painted a luminous white, with a magnificent gold altarpiece showing scenes from the life of St Catherine of Alexandria, to whom the cathedral is dedicated.

Visiting Old Goa

Allow at least half a day if you plan to visit all the main buildings in Old Goa. The churches, convents and cathedrals cover a considerable area, though no single building justifies a visit of more than about half an hour. Admission to all, including the Museum, was free at the time of writing. There are refreshment stands selling cold bottled drinks at the coach park on the main road and a small open-air café selling drinks and snacks in the grounds of the Se Cathedral.

▼ *Below: The Se Cathedral in Old Goa dates from 1562, the earliest era of the Portuguese conquest.*

▶ *Right: The interior of the Church of St Francis of Assisi is elaborately decorated with scenes from the saint's life.*

Church of St Francis of Assisi ★
This is the best-preserved of all Old Goa's great churches. The façade of the church, built in 1661, is three-tiered, with an eight-sided tower on each side. The main entrance is decorated with circular pilasters and a band of rosettes and is the only remaining link to the original building, dating from 1521. It is also the only surviving piece in Asia of the characteristic Manueline church design of 16th-century Portugal. Inside, the nave is barrel-vaulted and the choir is supported by a rib-vaulted crossing. The internal buttress walls are frescoed with floral designs. Above the tabernacle is a large statue of St Francis with Christ on the Cross. Below are statues of St Peter and St Paul. Painted panels on the walls of the nave show scenes from the life of St Francis. Much of the original interior was heavily gilded and painted, and enough of it remains to give some inkling of its glory.

Luíz Vaz de Camões

Luís Vaz de Camões, whose statue is displayed on the ground floor of the Archaeological Museum, arrived in Goa in 1554 as an itinerant soldier and served under the Viceroys of Goa for 16 years, fighting on the Malabar (now Kerala) coast, in Malacca and in Indo-China. In these years he composed his epic poem cycle, *Os Lusiadas*, the greatest work of Portuguese literature. Though the Portuguese erected the statue here in his honour, his work hardly mentions Goa.

Old Goa Archaeological Museum ★★
The museum is in the former **Convent of St Francis of**

Assisi, between the **Church of St Francis** and the **Se Cathedral**. Its collection depicts the history of Goa before and during the Portuguese period. There are stone slabs and statues from the era of Hindu rule, paintings of Vasco da Gama, Afonso de Albuquerque and later Portuguese grandees, and coins minted by Portuguese, Muslim, and Hindu rulers of Goa. Among the most striking exhibits is a stone carving of Vishnu, his consort Lakshmi and his mount, the half-man, half-bird Garuda. Open 10:00–17:00, except Fridays and holidays; UNESCO World Heritage Sites video showing 10:30, 13:00 and 15:30, www.asi.nic.in

Basilica of Bom Jesus ★★

Opposite the Se Cathedral complex, the basilica church of Good Jesus, built by the Jesuits and consecrated in 1605, is a mixture of lavish gilt and silver with fading paint and crumbling plaster. Outside, exposed red laterite blocks, once stuccoed, and huge buttresses lend an impression of massive solidity. The Baroque west front is its most striking feature. Within, the tomb of **St Francis Xavier** is Goa's holiest relic. Elaborately carved in jasper and decorated by fine bronze plaques depicting scenes from the saint's life, it was given to the church by the Duke of Tuscany, in 1698. The saint lies in a battered solid silver casket.

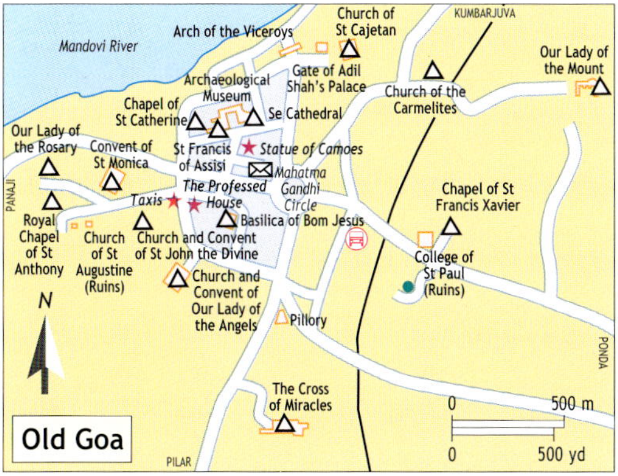

St Francis Xavier

The Spanish-born Francisco Xavier (1506–1552) was one of the founders of the Jesuit order and in 1542 was sent to Asia by the King of Portugal to Christianize the Portuguese colonies in India. He spent three years in southern India before travelling east to the Portuguese colony of Malacca (now Melaka in Malaysia) and Japan. He died in 1552 while trying to reach China and was buried first in Malacca, then disinterred and his remains brought back to Goa. His embalmed relics are preserved in a huge silver sarcophagus and are displayed at intervals, generally every 10 years. It was last shown in 2004.

▶ *Right: Cool, white colonnades surround the inner courtyard of the Professed House.*

The Professed House ★

The Professed House, the home of the Jesuit order, is cool and quiet. In a corner of the deserted second-floor gallery stands a wooden effigy of a saint, minus its head, which is gradually being eroded by woodworm. The building is still used by the order as a seminary.

Building Materials

The dilapidated state of many of Goa's colonial-era buildings is mainly due to the use of laterite which does not weather well. The Portuguese solution was to cover the stonework with a protective layer of painted plaster. This required regular maintenance and replacement and after the buildings were eventually abandoned, the monsoon rains wreaked havoc.

Chapel of St Catherine ★★

This is Old Goa's newest and oldest church. The first chapel was founded by **Afonso de Albuquerque** in 1510. After many additions and subsequent enlargements, the building was completely rebuilt in 1952.

Convent of St Monica ★★

The convent complex was built between 1637–45 on the site of an earlier convent which was destroyed by fire in 1636. One of the most imposing buildings in Old Goa, it is surprisingly plain inside. Built on a square plan around a central courtyard, the three-storey structure is supported by substantial buttresses both inside and out. The building is now the home of the **Mater Dei Institute**, set up to encourage the study of theology by nuns.

Church and Convent of St John the Divine ★

Close to the Convent of St Monica in the section of Old Goa called the **Holy Hill**, the Convent of St John was one of the religious foundations abandoned in 1835 and later passed into the hands of the Convent of St Monica. It was built in 1685 and restored by the Portuguese government in 1961. It is now a Franciscan nunnery.

Church of Our Lady of the Rosary ★

This is the oldest church in Old Goa to remain intact. From this spot Albuquerque commanded his troops in the crucial battle for Goa in 1510, and in gratitude for victory built a church which was replaced by the present one in 1549. The church is open only on feast days.

Church of St Cajetan ★★★

Built between 1656–61, this large church's façade is based on the original design of **St Peter's** in Rome. The interior is domed and embellished by seven gilt altarpieces. The church is still in use as a religious college, and following several restorations the building is one of the best preserved of Goa's great religious foundations. Rich wooden carvings on the altar and pulpit are particularly attractive. In the centre of the church is a well which is sometimes claimed to be evidence that St Cajetan's stands on the site of an earlier Hindu temple.

Church of St Augustine ★

Two walls of a massive 46m (150ft) belfry mark the colossal wreck of the Church of St Augustine. Built in 1602, the church is now reduced to a maze of shattered black laterite walls around a flagged floor set with 17th-century Portuguese tombstones.

Royal Chapel of St Anthony

The Chapel of St Anthony in Old Goa is often called the Royal Chapel. As the patron saint of Portugal, St Anthony was highly regarded. His statue held the rank of captain, and on St Anthony's Day each year the statue was paraded to the colonial treasury to receive its salary, which went into the coffers of the Augustinian order.

Carnival

The biggest event of the year in Panaji is carnival, held during the four days preceding Lent. The high point of the celebration is a parade of decorated floats accompanied by rival troops of up to 100 brightly constumed dancers. There is keen competition among local groups for each year's carnival prize. Daytime celebrations are followed by dancing every evening.

Royal Chapel of St Anthony ★

This small chapel next to the ruined Church of St Augustine was dedicated to Portugal's patron saint, and built in the early 16th century. Like its neighbour, it was controlled by the **Augustinian** order and abandoned when the order was dissolved in Portuguese lands in 1835. The building was restored in 1894 and again, like several other buildings on the site, in 1961. Next to the shell of the ruined St Augustine's, it looks almost brand new.

Arch of the Viceroys ★★

The triumphal arch astride the road leading to the Mandovi waterfront is a 1954 restoration of the original arch, which fell down in 1948. The road which passed through the arch was Goa's main thoroughfare, with the **Viceregal Palace** to its left. The original arch was commissioned in 1599 by Francisco da Gama, grandson of the great navigator and governor of Goa in the late 16th century. It was originally a ceremonial entrance to the city from the main anchorage on the Mandovi, and the side facing the river is therefore the most striking. The statue of **Vasco da Gama** which stands within the arch is a clumsy modern replacement of the 16th-century original. The deer carved into the laterite stonework are a memento of his coat of arms.

Gate of the Adil Shah's Palace ★

In front of St Cajetan's Church, a flight of six stone steps leads to a rectangular, decorated stone gateway, the only surviving remnant of the **Palace of the Adil Shah** of Bijapur who ruled the area before the coming of the Portuguese. After the Portuguese conquest, the palace was taken over as the Viceregal residence. When the Viceroys moved their seat from fever-stricken Old Goa, the palace was demolished and its timber and building stone were used to build a new one at Panaji. The archway shows signs of Hindu workmanship and was probably looted from a Hindu temple by the Muslim builders.

Church of St Paul of the Arches ★

All that survives of this 16th-century church is the stone arch of its main door. It was part of the **College of St Paul**, founded to train Hindu converts as Christian preachers, and was one of the first of Old Goa's churches to fall victim to the city's many epidemics. Consecrated in 1543, it was abandoned in 1570 and left to crumble until the 1830s, when it was demolished for building material. The nearby **Chapel of St Francis Xavier**, where the missionary saint is said to have prayed during his sojourn in Goa, was restored from its ruined state in 1884.

GOA VELHA AND SURROUNDS

Do not confuse this village, with its scattering of Portuguese-era religious buildings, with Old Goa. Goa Velha, about 16km (10 miles) southeast of Panaji, is on the southern edge of what was once the great colonial city between the Zuari and Mandovi rivers, while Old Goa is some 12km (7½ miles) to the north. Hardly any traces of the old city remain, but there are a couple of sights worth seeing near the present-day village which still bears the old Portuguese name of Goa Velha.

Place names

Goan place names and maps can be confusing. There are frequently two or more variations of each name in use, one dating from Portuguese days and one or more recent ethnic versions. Don't confuse the historic site of Old Goa with Goa Velha, several kilometres south. Be careful, too, not to mix up the resorts of Candolim (Kandoli) in northern Goa with Cansaulim in the south. Be aware that Bicholim and Dicholi are the same place, and that Mapusa in the north is also called Mapuca.

◀ *Left: Glowing stained-glass windows illuminate the interior of the Pilar Seminary.*

▲ *Above: A panoramic view of Goa's ancient churches.*

Pilar Seminary ★

The seminary complex north of Goa Velha was founded as a **Capuchin** convent in 1613, abandoned in 1835 and restored by the **Carmelite** order in 1858. It is now in the hands of the **St Francis Xavier Missionary Society**. Its most attractive building is the monastic church, with its magnificent Baroque doorway. The seminary stands on a low hill, and is worth a visit not just in its own right but also for the view of the Zuari and of the site of the former Old Goa inland.

Church of St Anne ★

The Church of St Anne, about 3km (2 miles) north of Goa Velha in the hamlet of **Tallauli** (Talaulim), is one of the grandest religious buildings outside the precincts of Old Goa. Its five-storey façade is unkempt, but the interior is gracefully vaulted, whitewashed and cool. The church was consecrated in 1695, replacing an earlier building dating from the 16th century. It is unlikely to be open except on Sundays and on feast days.

Vasco Da Gama

Vasco da Gama set sail from Lisbon in July 1497 to pioneer a trade route around the **Cape of Good Hope** to India and the spice islands of the east. With a fleet of four ships and 170 men, he rounded the Cape in December, then sailed up the east African coast, crossing the Indian Ocean to land at **Calicut**, in Kerala, on May 20, 1498. This first European expedition to the east opened the way for almost five centuries of Portuguese rule in Asia.

MORMUGAO PROVINCE

Vasco da Gama ★

Named after the famous Portuguese navigator and known universally as just Vasco, this small, busy commercial centre is everything Panaji isn't. It is dominated by freight and import-export businesses, with no historic buildings or sights of interest. The arrival of express trains from out of state adds a brief flurry of excitement several times a day. **Vasco** is of interest only as a transport terminus for those arriving or leaving Goa by rail or looking for bus transport to the southern provinces of Goa or points south.

Mormugao ★

This is one of the best natural harbours on India's west coast, rivalled only by Mumbai and by Kochi in Kerala. Under Portuguese rule it was of little importance, but since union with India it has become Goa's most important seaport and is also used by the Indian Navy. Many tours of southern and central Goa include a brief stop at Mormugao or a visit to its seaport, through which millions of tons of iron ore are exported each year, and which is one of western India's biggest oil refineries. Many visitors may be surprised to find these included in their itinerary, but India still takes considerable pride in such symbols of progress and industrial development. A passenger ferry service across the mouth of the Zuari connects Mormugao with Dona Paula, on the north shore.

Bogmalo ★★

This beach, only 3km (2 miles) south of Dabolim airport, was naturally one of the first in Goa to be developed for tourism. It is dominated by Goa's first and most obtrusive luxury hotel at its southern end and surrounded by a gaggle of beachside restaurants, bars and souvenir stores along the sandy crescent of beach. Comparatively small by Goan standards – a mere 1km (600yd) from end to end – Bogmalo, despite its restricted size and the presence of the large hotel complex, does not feel unduly over-developed. The beach is a favourite for day visitors from Vasco da Gama and is also conveniently close to Panaji.

Taxi Tips

If you are travelling on a package holiday a coach and tour operator representative will be waiting to meet you at Dabolim airport. Independent travellers should head for the official taxi desk, where you pay in advance and are given a slip of paper to hand to your driver. If you are on a tight budget, take a taxi to Vasco da Gama, 5km (3 miles) from the airport, where you can connect with bus and rail services.

PANAJI AND CENTRAL GOA AT A GLANCE

Best Times to Visit

The coolest months are from **December** to **March**. The hottest, driest months are during April and May. June and July should be avoided. The later monsoon months of **August** and **September** are better because this is when the rains slacken and the land is verdant. This can be a delightful time to visit.

Getting There

Goa's international airport at Dabolim is a 45-minute drive from Panaji; fixed-fare taxis operate from the airport to points throughout Goa. When this edition was researched construction of a new international airport at Mopa in northern Goa had been delayed yet again. It is unlikely to open before 2020. It is planned that it will be used in tandem with the airport at Dabolim. **Trains** to southern Goa and Karnataka leave from Vasco da Gama station. The 760km (500-mile) coastal Konkan Railway, completed in 1998, connects Vasco and other Goan stations (Pernem, Karmali, Thivim and Margao) with Mumbai in the north and Ernakulam in Kerala, halving journey time between Mumbai and Goa to 10 hours. There are direct services to Bengaluru, taking about 20 hours. In 2004, non-stop express services were introduced between Margao and Delhi. Buses for southern Goa also leave from Vasco da Gama. **Buses** to and from northern Goa leave from the Pato bus terminal, east of Panaji town centre. Interstate bus travel is not recommended. **Ferry service** from Mumbai has been suspended for several years. Ferries may resume in 2015 but don't count on it.

Getting Around

Cars with a driver can be hired from local and international car hire companies, hotels and from the Goa Department of Tourism. Self-drive hire is not advisable. **Taxis** can be chartered by the day to explore the region and other parts of Goa, either by negotiating a price with the driver directly or, more easily and usually no more expensively, through a hotel or tour agency. Tourist taxis, usually cream or white, are booked by the journey, or by the hour or day through your hotel. Black and yellow ordinary taxis are officially metered, though persuading the driver to use the meter is difficult. Agree a fare before boarding if possible. **Auto-rickshaws**, three wheeled scooters with a covered bench seat behind the driver, are more expensive than taxis and are used only for short hops. Public **buses** are frequent but quite slow; longer journeys require several changes. Buses are open, so journeys are breezy but dusty. Air conditioned tour buses and minibuses can be chartered by groups through local tour agencies. The road journey between Vasco and Panaji involves a long detour to the first bridge across the Zuari. Passenger **ferries** go between Mormugao and Dona Paula.

Where to Stay

Panaji offers a range of accommodation from basic backpacker's hotels to a number of mid-range, locally owned properties. There is no accommodation in Old Goa.

Luxury

Cidade de Goa, Vainguinim Beach, Dona Paula, tel: 0832 245 4545, www.cidadedegoa.com A self-contained, somewhat isolated resort on a rather unimpressive small beach.

Panjim Pousada, 31st January Road, Panaji, tel: 0832 222 8318, www.panjiminn.com Acclaimed small boutique hotel with nine rooms in the former mansion of a wealthy Hindu family.

Mid-range

Hotel La Paz Gardens, Swatantra Path, Vasco da Gama, tel: 0832 2512 121, www.hotellapazgardens.com Vasco's largest, most modern hotel.

Panjim People's, 31st January Road, Fontainhas, Panaji, tel: 0832 222 6523, www.panjiminn.com Same management as Panjim Inn next door. Comfortable rooms with antique beds in a converted former schoolhouse.

Hotel Mandovi, PO Box 164, D. B. Bandodkar Marg, Panaji, tel: 0832 222 4405, www.hotelmandovigoa.com

In Panjim centre; recently renovated, comfortable, modern.
Hotel Nova Goa, Dr Atmaram Borkar Road, Panaji, tel: 0832 222 6231, www.hotelnovagoa.com Three-star value, with pool, gym and business centre.

Budget

Panjim Inn, E-212, 31st January Rd, Fontainhas, Panaji, tel: 0832 222 6523, www.panjiminn.com Family-run hotel with carved wooden four-posters, fans, mosquito nets and balconies. Overlooks courtyard of 300-year-old Portuguese home.
Afonso Guest House, Rua São Sebastian, Panaji, tel: 0832 222 2359. Clean, airy en-suite rooms; some with balconies and air conditioning.

Where to Eat

Note that small restaurants may be called 'hotels', though they have no bedrooms attached.

Panaji

Goa's capital does not have as many restaurant options as the state's popular beach resorts. For evening meals, the best bet is to head for a hotel.

Hotel Venite, Post Office Road, Fontainhas. Not a hotel but a delightful old-fashioned restaurant on the first floor, with wrought-iron balconies and polished wooden floors. The most atmospheric place to eat and drink in Panaji.
Riorico, Hotel Mandovi (*see* Where to Stay). Goan food.
Quarterdeck Restaurant, Mandovi Park, Panaji, tel: 0832 243 2904. Informal open-air terrace overlooking river, opposite Hotel Mandovi. Seafood, soft drinks, cold beer. Open daytime and evenings.
Panjim Inn (*see* Where to Stay), Garden, balcony, fresh juices and good seafood.
Confeitaria, 31st January Rd, Panaji, tel: 0832 2222 5791. For a change from Indian food, sample Portuguese-style pastries at this small café.

Vasco

The restaurants of Hotel La Paz Garden offer a choice of Indian, Goan, Chinese and European-style cuisine.

Old Goa

A small outdoor café in the grounds of the Se Cathedral sells soft drinks and snacks in the shade of a huge tree.

Bogmalo

A surprisingly good choice of small seafood restaurants offering excellent value. Most of them cluster beside the semi-permanent market village at the south end of the beach.

Shopping

The Municipal Market in Panaji is where locals shop for household essentials and nests of shiny tiffin tins, cheap glittery jewellery and retro Indian-style luggage make good souvenirs. More chic shops include:
Wendell Rodricks, Luis Gomes Gardens, Panaji, tel: 0832 2238 1777, www.wendellrodricks.com Stylish silk, cotton, linen clothes for men and women.
Sangolda Nilaya Home Collection, Chgomi Road, Sangolda, tel: 0832 240 9309. Expensive but gorgeous household fabrics, furniture and accessories.

Tours and Excursions

Goa Tourist Development Corporation bookings, tel: 0832 243 8866, www.goa-tourism.com Sightseeing tours from Panaji and Vasco, including day tours to north and south Goa, Old Goa, Ponda, the Dudhsagar waterfalls and the Bondla and Bhagwan Mahavir Wildlife Sanctuaries. Also one-hour **cruises**, and half-day trips on Mandovi and Zuari rivers.
Travel Corporation India, Citicentre 19, Patto Plaza, Panjim, tel: 0832 663 9148, www.tcindia.com River and canal cruises, barbecues, temple and wildlife tours.
The Golden Chariot, a luxury train with sleeping cars, bar and restaurant, and sightseeing cars, runs between Goa and Bengaluru, www.goldenchariottrain.com

Useful Contacts

Government of Goa Tourist Information Office, Tourist Home, Patto, Panaji, tel: 0832 222 5583. Leaflets, maps, list of hotels and guesthouses, bookings for state-run hotels and wildlife reserve bungalows, excursions and ferry bookings.

4
Northern Goa

The **beaches** of northern Goa between the Mandovi River in the south and the Chapora River in the north are the most popular in the state. There are a string of hotels stretching up the coast from the ramparts of the 17th-century Portuguese **Fort Aguada** almost as far as the 18th-century stronghold at **Chapora**, overlooking **Vagator** beach and village. Most of these hotels cater to a mixed British, northern European and Indian clientele. Fort Aguada itself happens to be one of the most expensive hotels in Goa. Most of the beaches along this part of the coast are long stretches of bright golden sand, backed by palms which mask the hotel buildings. Most Goan coastal villages stand some distance from the high water line, helping to preserve the illusion of an untouched tropical paradise. During the monsoon season, between mid-June and the end of August, the beaches are less attractive. Heavy surf removes much of the sand, the small shacks and bars close down, and frequent torrential downpours send people scurrying for cover.

North of the Chapora River, development is far less extensive, and the region's emptier beaches and simple village facilities attracts budget-conscious independent travellers and long-stay visitors seeking an escape from the crowds. Rocky headlands split by most of the beaches along Goa's far north coast are smaller than those south of the Chapora, with small villages hidden away by coconut palms inland.

Don't Miss

*** **Fort Aguada:** massive medieval bastions enclose five-star hotels and a fine secluded beach.
*** **Anjuna:** fantastic stretch of uncrowded beach, a small, relaxed village and a lively weekly market.
** **Chapora:** 16th-century hilltop fortress stands on a headland overlooking fine beaches.
** **Vagator:** uncrowded coves of golden sand.

◀ *Opposite: The palm-fringed white sand coves of Vagator.*

Beach Etiquette

Indian tourists flock to Goa's hippy beaches in the hope of catching a glimpse of naked Western flesh, and it is not unusual to see a respectable Indian trying to persuade a topless western girl to pose with him for a souvenir photo. Though many young visitors wear the absolute minimum on the beach, displays of public nudity are technically illegal and very much frowned on by local people. Modesty is a way of life for Indians of all castes and religions.

Fort Aguada ★★★

During the early 17th century, the Portuguese turned this northern headland of the **Mandovi** into a powerful fortress to control the mouth of the river. In 1612 they cut a channel across the neck of the headland between the Mandovi and the smaller **Nerul River** to the north, making Aguada into an artificial island. Throughout the period of Portuguese conquest and consolidation it proved impregnable from both sea and land. From its walls, 79 great guns raked every approach and commanded the entrance to the Mandovi.

Massive laterite walls and bastions surround the island, some of them in good repair, others crumbling into ruin. On the north shore at the mouth of the Nerul, the battlements overlook a small fishing harbour, while a circular bastion-jetty, jutting out to sea, effectively cuts off the beach immediately in front of the island from the much longer stretch of sand to the north. The outer fortress walls, entered by a bridge across the currently dry moat, now contain several of Goa's top luxury resort complexes, none of them too obtrusive thanks to the surrounding palms and other greenery.

Just inside the main gateway of the citadel is Aguada's most prominent landmark, the squat 13m (42ft) white tower of the **lighthouse** built in 1864. Above it, on the highest point of the headland, is the pretty little church of **St Lawrence**, patron saint of sailors, which was built in 1630.

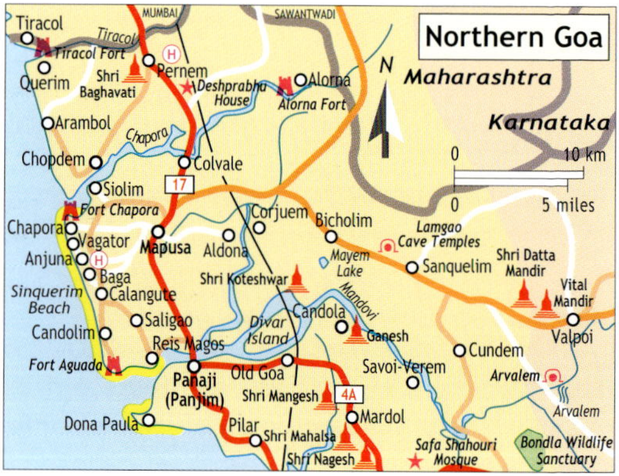

The main citadel of the fortress also houses guests, but not willing ones. It is used as a **prison**. So is another Portuguese fortress, **Reis Magos**, some 9km (5½ miles) east of Aguada on the north coast of the Mandovi. Next to its grim walls stands the **Church of Reis Magos** (Church of the Magi Kings), built in 1555 and restored during the 18th century. The steps to the church are guarded by carved stone lions, probably looted from an earlier Hindu temple, and the royal coat of arms of Portugal is carved above the door.

FORT AGUADA TO THE CHAPORA

Sinquerim beach sweeps north from Fort Aguada in an unbroken stretch of sand terminating in a rocky headland at the end of **Baga** beach. The villages of **Candolim**, **Calangute** and **Baga**, which are strung out along this beach, have grown

◀ *Left: Bastions stretch into the sea at Fort Aguada, one of north Goa's most expensive resorts.*

into popular holiday resorts. The main attraction of each of these is the beach, but a few pretty churches dating from the 17th and 18th centuries lend some historic and architectural interest to the area. The northern stretch of coast beyond Baga has so far escaped full-scale tourist development. This area was the first of Goa's 1960s hippy havens, but with the growth of more orthodox package tourism the counter-culture has moved on to more remote strands in the far north and deep south.

Northern Goa is less well endowed with sights to see than the central provinces. The beach is the main attraction, while inland the countryside is a mixture of seemingly endless paddy fields and coconut groves. Beach life for visitors centres on swimming and sunbathing with few of the powered water sports such as waterskiing or parascending. This is mainly because of the prohibitive cost of importing equipment. Relaxation, however, is what most visitors are after, and relaxation is what this stretch of coast delivers supremely well – whether in the luxury hotels and package holiday resorts on the southern stretch of the coast or in the simple budget-traveller encampments to the north. A host of informal services have sprung up to make beach life even more relaxing. Fruit vendors bring you slices of pineapple or drinking coconuts, while masseurs offer to relieve your aches and pains. Cold drink vendors, jewellery pedlars and the occasional furtive marijuana dealer will also stroll by. Beach business is an entertainment in itself.

Water Sports

Goa's beaches offer a limited choice of water sports, as importing and maintaining powered equipment is quite expensive. **Water-skiing** and **jetskis** are available at major resorts though, including those at Fort Aguada. **Scuba** training and dive trips are also offered at Calangute. Water sports are not available during the monsoon season.

Candolim (Kandoli) ★★

Not to be confused with Cansaulim in southern Goa, the first resort settlement north of Aguada is situated about 400m (1312ft) inland from the shore. Newer hotel and restaurant buildings surround the mid-17th-century **Church of Our Lady of Hope**. The church is typically grandiose, and seems far too large for the tiny fishing and farming village Candolim was before the coming of tourism. Its tall decorative towers – a later 18th-century addition – dominate the village.

Calangute (Kalangut) ★

North of Candolim, Calangute is about 1km (2/3 mile) inland, at the crossroads of the main north–south route and the coastal road to **Baga** and **Calangute** beach. The resort is the biggest and most popular in northern Goa, despite its steeply shelving beach. Much of its sand is stripped away during the monsoon, but is gradually replaced throughout the winter. Water sports are plentiful, as are beach pedlars, who can be irritatingly persistent. The newer holiday village, with its hotels and bars, merges imperceptibly into the older settlement. Like Candolim, Calangute is built around a decorative Portuguese church, dedicated to St Alex and faced by an elaborate artificial grotto.

▼ *Below: FIshing boats on the river at Calangute.*

PARTY TIME

Anjuna is famed for its full moon parties, when hundreds of young ravers from all over the world gather to hear the latest in dance music played by DJs from Europe's trendiest nightspots. Each party is an all-night, high-decibel event, and you can find out when and where the next one will be held by asking around in the more relaxed beach bars. If it's too loud, you're too old.

Saligao ★

The village of Saligao, 2km (1¼ miles) east of Calangute, is poised to merge with the larger settlement in the fairly near future, with building already spilling over the coastal highway. Saligao is worth the short detour from Calangute for a look at its lovely, white-painted **Church of the Rosary**. Built in 1873, it is in a sharp-edged, angular neo-Gothic style which sets it apart from the Baroque or Manueline churches which are more commonly seen in Goa's towns and villages.

Baga ★★★

This is the northernmost resort village on **Sinquerim** and has the best beach north of Aguada. Baga is sheltered by a headland which cuts it off from the smaller, more intimate

▶ *Right: Anjuna, with its idyllic sandy coves separated by rocky headlands, is where the 'real' Goa begins.*

beaches of the Anjuna–Vagator area to the north. A mixture of good-value, mid-market hotels and restaurants makes it a popular package holiday resort. However, the flotilla of wooden fishing boats hauled up on the beach or moored offshore is a reminder of the old, traditional way of life of the village. The hotels and restaurants are spread out along the main highway, which runs only 100m (330ft) from the beach. Baga also offers other options: walk south to the bigger choice of restaurants and water sports at **Calangute**, or north over the headland to the less developed beaches of **Anjuna** and **Vagator**.

Anjuna ★★★

Large-scale tourism development comes to an abrupt halt north of the Baga headland, and many people would argue that this is where the 'real' Goa starts. Anjuna village and its sprawling collection of cheap accommodation and eating places are favoured more by backpackers and other independents rather than by the mainstream holiday-makers. Despite the beginnings of more middle-of-the-road development, the atmosphere remains very different from that of Baga or Calangute – reminiscent in fact of a more-or-less continuous alternative lifestyle festival. This is interrupted only by the monsoon, when the counter-culture crowds head back to Europe, Australia or the USA, to return when the rain stops in September. Anjuna comes into its own once a month for its famous (or notorious) **full moon party**, an institution since the 1970s, when everyone heads for the beach for a night of raving and loud music. If you intend to join the festivities, be aware that the crowd is always infiltrated by plain-clothed Indian policemen keen to improve their arrest record.

Anjuna's other major event is the **weekly flea market**, held each Wednesday. You are unlikely to find anything here that you have not been offered in village shops or by beach vendors, but it is a great place to go for a morning's one-stop shopping for all your holiday souvenirs and gifts. The main stock in trade is brightlycoloured garments and glittering jewellery from all

Drugs

Goa's beaches have been a byword for soft drugs, mainly **bhang** and **hashish**, since the 1960s. With the growth in mainstream tourism, local authorities have become even keener to prosecute drug users. Drug dealers who approach potential customers on the beach, on the street or in cheap accommodation often double as police informers. Possession of even small amounts is punishable by long prison sentences.

over India and – because competition between vendors is intense – you are in a better bargaining position than when you are haggling one-to-one with a beach pedlar.

Bargaining Tips

Hard bargaining is the rule in markets like those at **Mapusa** or on the beach at **Anjuna**. You may find you will be able to negotiate a better bulk price for several items than by negotiating for each purchase separately. At the beach market, you should be able to bring the asking price down by anywhere from 30 to 60%, but at Mapusa don't expect to squeeze more than 10% off.

Vagator ★★

A track leads over the hill north of Anjuna village to the attractive beaches of Vagator. The two golden sand coves are separated by rugged black reefs. Tiny shacks line the beach, competing to play the latest and loudest dance music day and night on battery-powered sound systems. The clientele is young and on a small budget, and some people camp on the slopes above the beach.

Chapora ★★

Overlooking the Vagator coves atop a bare hill of black laterite boulders stands the grim-looking **Fort Chapora**. Its ring of ramparts, studded with Portuguese-domed bastions, dates from the 18th century, when the Portuguese built a chain of forts to link and defend their Indian territories. An earlier Muslim fortress, known as **Shapur**, belonged to the Adil Shah, the last Muslim ruler of Goa. There is nothing to see inside the walls other than the bastions on each side which offer fine views south along the sweeping beaches towards Fort Aguada and north over the estuary of the **Chapora River**.

Chapora village is on the south bank of the river, east of the fort and sheltered from the sea by the headland on which the fort stands. A fair-sized fishing fleet anchors in this safe natural harbour, and Chapora is still a fishing village with a little low-budget tourism, not a former village turned full-scale resort.

Hippy Beaches

Goa's first hippies were the real thing. They arrived in India the hard way having travelled by bus, train or camper-van through Europe, Turkey, Iran, Afghanistan and Pakistan on the way. Today's hippies are young enough to be the children of the 60s hippies and many of them probably are. Most of them, though, have flown to India direct and have a return ticket tucked away in their ruck-sacks along with a Visa card.

MAPUSA AND BEYOND THE CHAPORA

Beyond the Chapora River, in **Pernem** province, lies Goa's longest stretch of undeveloped beach, protected from mass tourism by its inaccessibility. Getting there involves a long journey inland to the first crossing of the Chapora at **Colvale**, or a trip on the ferry between Siolim, 5km (3 miles) upriver from Chapora, and **Chopdem** on the north bank.

Mapusa ★

Some 20km (12½ miles) inland from Chapora, Mapusa is the main town of **Bardez** province and the main transport junction for travel to the Vagator area and points north of the river.

Mapusa Friday Market ★

Mapusa is the venue for one of Goa's biggest produce markets. Held each Friday and well worth a visit, it draws buyers and vendors from all over northern and central Goa. The contrast between this busy market selling everyday household goods and all sorts of fruit, vegetables, fish, herbs and spices and the Wednesday market which is geared towards tourists at Anjuna could not be greater. Visit early in the morning to see the thronged market at its liveliest.

Church of Our Lady of Miracles ★

Consecrated in 1594, the church has a fine baroque front which is deceptively modern. It has been rebuilt many times, most recently in 1962 and was built on the site of an earlier Hindu temple. Mapusa is noted for its annual festival of Our Lady of Miracles, celebrated by Hindus and Christians alike on the first Sunday 16 weeks after Easter. Goan Christians hold it in honour of the **Virgin Mary** and Hindus in veneration of their virgin goddess **Lairaya**.

◀ *Left: The ruins of the Portuguese Fort Chapora.*

Dussehra

Dussehra, the Hindu festival held at the end of the rains every **October**, is a big date in Pernem, where temple images are paraded around the village square, adorned with marigold garlands. Dussehra begins on the 10th day of the new moon in October and continues for a week, with dancing, fireworks and festivities every night.

Pernem ★★

North of Mapusa on the main road, Pernem is the capital of Pernem province and the northernmost part of Goa. It is separated from the neighbouring state of Maharashtra by the Tiracol River. The village has several noteworthy and highly colourful Hindu temples.

Shri Bhagavati Temple ★★

The temple to Bhagavati, one of the destructive aspects of Shiva's spouse Parvati, is impossible to miss. Located along one side of the main square, it has lifesize stone elephants guarding its entrance. Within the temple, Bhagavati is represented by a massive statue carved from black basalt.

Mauli Temple ★

About 1km (2/3 mile) from Pernem, this small temple houses a black stone statue of the goddess Mauli and is prettily located beside the small Sarmal waterfall.

Deshprabhu House ★★

This rambling Hindu mansion is the most magnificent family home in Goa. The **Deshprabhu** family were aristocrats under Portuguese rule and the grandiose 19th-century building with its 16 inner courts is a token of their wealth and power. Not all courtyards are open to visitors. The first courtyard houses a family temple and a small museum with a collection which gives a fascinating insight into the life of an important land-owning Hindu family. The most striking pieces in the collection are the solid silver palanquins in which family retainers carried the Deshprabhu children to the temple on Hindu festivals. Open 10:00–17:00, except Fridays and holidays.

Arambol ★★

The superb, untouched beach stretches unbroken for 12km (7½ miles) from the mouth of the Chapora as far as this quintessential Goan fishing village and hippy hideaway. Arambol village is around 1km (½ mile) inland. Accommodation and facilities are extremely basic and are

▲ *Above: The tiny fort which guards the river mouth at Tiracol on Goa's northern border was built by the Portuguese.*

likely to remain so until improved access makes Arambol an attractive prospect to the hotel developers.

Tiracol ★★

This is Goa's last outpost in the north. A tiny Portuguese **fort**, dating from the 18th century when the Portuguese captured an earlier fortress from the local Raja, stands on a hillock guarding the river mouth. Within its ramparts is a small chapel to **St Anthony**. Formerly run as a hotel, the fort is not at present open to the public.

Alorna ★

Some 16km (10 miles) east of the main highway, on the southern tributary of the Chapora River, this small **fort** is one of the few inland strongholds built by the Portuguese. Its purpose was to defend the river crossing against **Maharatha** raiders from the north. Apart from the crumbling ramparts there is little to see.

BICHOLIM AND SURROUNDS

Bicholim province lies north of the Mandovi, east of the Mapusa River, and south of the state border with Maharashtra.

Markets

Markets like those to be found in most Goan towns are good places to shop for unusual **souvenirs**. Aromatic spices are good additions to your kitchen at home, and the stainless-steel tiffin tins with tight-fitting lids sold on many stalls are attractive storage containers. You can even buy a typical Indian tin suitcase, painted in bright floral patterns, to take your new purchases home in.

Tourism and Environment

Goa's tourism boom has been accused of damaging the environment, dispossessing local people from their land and pushing prices of food, land and housing beyond the reach of ordinary Goans. Pressure groups accuse the government of allowing hotels and restaurants to flout planning laws, and of condoning indiscriminate tourism development. Nevertheless, the government claims Goa's coastline will be able to absorb up to five million visitors a year by the second decade of the 21st century.

Bicholim (Dicholi) ★

Bicholim, the small main town of the province, is surrounded by a scattering of Hindu temples. The best way to visit these is with a hired car and a driver who is familiar with the district, as they are not signposted.

Shri Datta Mandir Temple ★

The 19th-century temple on the banks of the Mandovi is of unusual design, with a blue multi-tiered spire instead of the domed roof more common in Goan Hindu temples.

Vital Mandir Temple ★★

The local god Vital may date back to Dravidian times. His statue in this small temple is richly dressed, carved of local black laterite, and flanked by images of Lakshmi, consort of Vishnu, and Sarasvati, consort of Brahma.

Lamgao Cave Temples ★

These caves just outside Bicholim village can only be reached on foot. Both are Hindu holy places. The smaller cave contains a phallic lingam altar and a stone carving of the Nandi bull, the steed of Shiva. The caves are believed to have been dug originally by Buddhist monks and worshippers.

▼ Below: The chapel in Tiracol Fort served local villagers as well as the garrison.

Arvalem Caves and Waterfalls ★★

The earliest cave temples in Goa are in a series of rock outcrops southeast of the village of Sanquelim. Excavated some time between the third and the sixth centuries ad, each contains a Shiva lingam. Like those at Lamgao, they were probably the work of local Buddhists. A number of Buddha statues have been discovered in and around the area of Sanquelim village.

Best Times to Visit

See p. 54.

Getting There

Fort Aguada and Sinquerim resorts: buses (1–2 hours) depart from Panaji and Mapusa every hour. **Chapora, Vagator and Anjuna:** buses (1½ hours) from Panaji to **Mapusa**. Change buses at Mapusa or take an auto-rickshaw from Mapusa bus station. **Pernem:** Buses leave from Mapusa. To reach Arambol and the coast of Pernem province, take an auto-rickshaw from Pernem. **Bicholim and surrounds:** Buses arrive roughly every three hours from Mapusa. **By rail:** Konkan Railway operates daily between Thivim (for Mapusa), Karmali (for Panaji), Vasco (for Dabolim Airport), Margao, and north to Mumbai.

Getting Around

Visit Anjuna's Wed flea market by **fishing boat** from Baga or Calangute. **Taxis** and chauffeur-driven **cars** available through main resorts. **Auto-rickshaws** wait at bus stations (Mapusa and Bicholim).

Where to Stay

North of the Chapora there are few hotels, but plenty of small guesthouses and beach huts in and around Arambol.

Leena's Guesthouse, Girkar Warda, Arambol, tel: 0832 224 2926, www.leena-guesthouse.com Single and double rooms, some en-suite, near the beach.

Luxury

Vivanta by Taj Fort Aguada, Sinquerim, tel: 0832 664 5858, www.vivantabytaj.com Recently rebranded boutique-style resort; unique location inside old Portuguese fortress.

Nilaya Hermitage, Bhati, Arpora, Calangute, tel: 0832 226 9793, www.nilaya.com Boutique hotel; 11 rooms, beautifully decorated; stone buildings surrounding pool.

Mid-range

Laguna Anjuna, tel: 0832 227 4131, www.lagunaanjuna.com Resort hotel set in gardens; pool. On outskirts of Anjuna close to the beach.

Otter Creek Tents, tel: 0832 224 7616, www.aseascape.com Accommodation in permanent, comfortable tents (with en-suite bathroom) between river and sea and beach huts, also with en-suite facilities.

Lemon Tree Amarante Beach Resort, Vadi, Candolim, tel: 0832 398 8188 www.lemontreehotels.com Small hotel; pool, restaurant and en-suite rooms.

Budget

Palacete Rodrigues, Mazal Vaddo, Anjuna, tel: 0832 227 3358, www.palacetegoa.com Family-run guesthouse in restored 200-year-old mansion. Stylish, no pool and about 1.5km (1 mile) from the beach.

Hotel Bougainvillea Granpa's Inn, Gaunwaddi, Anjuna, tel: 0832 227 3270, www.granpasinn.com Rooms and suites surrounding a pool in a historic mansion with all mod cons. Some suites have private courtyards. Value for money.

Where to Eat

Sinquerim

Ganesh Shack, Candolim Beach. Family-run shack restaurant is a favourite with frequent visitors and serves excellent seafood.

Tito's, on Tito's Beach Road; daddy of the Baga/Calangute dining and entertainment scene and has grown into a small empire of clubs, bars, restaurants; karate school. Tel: 098239 29408, www.titosgroup.com

Anjuna

Vast choice of beach restaurants and food stalls.

Chapora

The main street is lined with small open-air restaurants and food stalls.

Mapusa

Ruta's World Cafe, St Xavier's Road, Mapusa, tel:0832 225 0757, www.caferuta.com This stylish cafe is the ideal spot for lunch, a snack or a glass of wine after shopping in Mapusa.

Spice Goa, Ground Floor, Satadhar Complex 3, tel: 0832 225 7148, www.spicegoa.com Good seafood restaurant on outskirts of Mapusa.

Pernem Province Beaches

The restaurant scene at the northernmost Goa beaches is even more informal than in Anjuna or Chapora.

Tours and Excursions

Unique Tours and Travels, Arpora, Calangute, tel: 0832 227 5086, www.goatravelmasti.com Day trips to spice plantations, dolphin-spotting cruises, bird-watching, longer tours beyond Goa's borders.

Useful Contacts

Directorate of Tourism, Tourist Shopping Complex, Mapusa, tel: 08322 262 390. Tourist info on the north and all of Goa.

5
Eastern Goa

Ponda, Sanguem and Satari, the landlocked provinces of central and eastern Goa, are often overlooked by visitors whose main focus is on the beaches and the sights of Panaji and Old Goa. Both Ponda and Sanguem offer different aspects of Goa, away from the holiday hotels and Portuguese churches and cathedrals. Added to the Portuguese empire much later than the coastal provinces, this part of Goa seems much more a part of India. Its landscapes, too, are different and more dramatic, with the forested slopes of the **Western Ghats** mountain range rising away from the coastal plain.

Ponda's attractions are mainly historic and man-made. The province is Goa's Hindu heartland, with the largest concentration of Hindu temples in the state, while on its eastern border the **Bondla Wildlife Sanctuary** offers a glimpse of Goa's wilder side. Ponda borders Tiswadi in the northwest and is separated from Bicholim by the upper reaches of the **Mandovi River**, while the **Upper Zuari River** divides it from Mormugao and Salcete in the west. The easiest way to explore Ponda is with a car and driver hired at your holiday base, but there are also a number of tours which take in the high points of its Hindu temples, with or without a visit to Bondla.

Sanguem province is long and thin, bordering the provinces of Satari to the north and Ponda, Salcete, Quepem and Canacona to the west. To the east, the ranges of the Western Ghats divide it from Karnataka state. Sanguem is tailormade for rail travel, with Goa's main railway line from Vasco da Gama to Karnataka and points east cutting across

Don't Miss

*** **Ponda:** colourful Hindu temples are scattered around this picturesque region.
*** **Tambdi Surla Temple:** ancient Hindu temple, hidden away among wooded hills.
** **Bhagwan Mahavir Wildlife Sanctuary:** offers excellent bird watching and game drives.
** **Dudhsagar Falls:** interesting train ride through spectacular scenery.

◀ *Opposite: The Shri Shantadurga Temple, dating back almost four centuries, shows its Portuguese influences.*

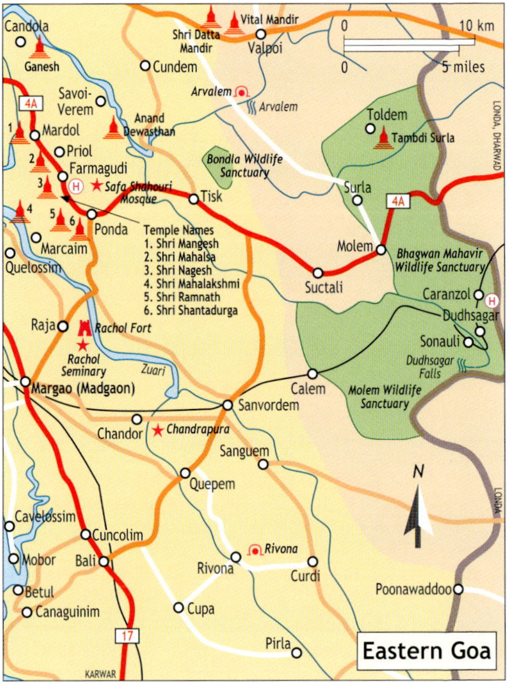

the province and winding its way through the passes of the Western Ghats to the Karnataka plateau across the state border.

The province's main attractions are natural, and conveniently close to the railway line. They include the impressive **Dudhsagar Falls**, one of India's highest waterfalls. Near the village of **Molem** is the second of Goa's wildlife sanctuaries, and at **Tambdi Surla** one of Goa's oldest Hindu temples survives.

Satari, the third of the inland provinces, borders Bicholim in the west and Sanguem in the south, with the state borders of Maharashtra and Karnataka on its north and east sides. Those keen to get off the beaten track will find that the province has something to offer. Getting to the main town of **Valpoi** will require several bus changes or your own transport.

PONDA

During the first two centuries of the Portuguese conquest, all temples and mosques in Portuguese territory were destroyed. By the time Ponda came under Portuguese rule in 1764 there was greater toleration, and its temples have survived, though almost all have been rebuilt and restored so many times that nothing remains of the original building. Most are within an 8km (5 mile) radius of Ponda village.

Hindu temples follow the same pattern throughout Goa, and many visitors may feel that a visit to more than one is overdoing it. Frequent restoration, repainting and rebuilding means that, despite their age, they impress the foreigner with little sense of history and none of the grandeur of the echoing, empty and dilapidated Portuguese cathedrals.

Driving in India

Both chauffeur-driven and self-drive car hire are available from major international chains in India. When driving, bear in mind that roads are often poorly maintained and traffic can be intimidating, with diesel-belching trucks, buses, jeeps and taxis jockeying for position. Hazards unique to India include sacred cows, which hold up traffic and woe betide the driver who collides with one! Roads are also haphazardly signposted so navigation can be a problem. It's better to hire a driver who knows the roads. Chauffeur-driven hire cars are among India's travel bargains.

Shri Nagesh Temple ★★

This temple, 1km (½ mile) from the village of **Farmagudi** on the main Ponda road, is more brightly coloured than many local shrines, with vividly painted gods and demons around the base of its squat tower. A black stone slab mounted in the wall dates the temple from at least the early 15th century. An effigy of the Nandi bull, the mount of Shiva, stands outside the entrance to the temple hall. Nagesh is an aspect of Shiva, and the temple contains several lingam and mukhalingam shrines.

Shri Shantadurga Temple ★★★

There has been a temple to Shri Shantadurga – an aspect of Parvati – near **Kavalem**, just outside Ponda town, for at least four centuries, but the existing one clearly shows the Portuguese influence which had begun to alter the design of local temples by that time.

It is the largest of Ponda's temples and attracts many pilgrims on Hindu holy days. Two towers overlook a huge flagged courtyard. The doors to the shrine are heavily decorated in silver, and within stands a marble statue of Shantadurga accompanied by images of Shiva and Vishnu (*see* www.shreeshantadurga.com).

Ancient and Modern

Most of Goa's Hindu temples stand on centuries-old sites, but the temples themselves look remarkably modern compared with the crumbling cathedrals of Old Goa. Temples are frequently refurbished, repainted and even completely rebuilt, though they may contain very ancient images of the gods. An exception is the **Shri Mahadeva Temple** at Tambdi Surla, which has been long abandoned.

Shri Ramnath Temple ★★★

Only 100m (330ft) from the Shri Shantadurga Temple, the Shri Ramnath Temple is dedicated to **Shiva**. Its inner hall is one of the most lavishly decorated in the region, with embossed silver on the wall of the sanctuary and elaborate friezes and reliefs surrounding the entrance arch and supporting columns (*see* www.ramnathi.com).

Shri Mahalakshmi Temple ★

This temple near **Bandora**, about 5km (3 miles) from Ponda, is dedicated to **Lakshmi**. Its doors are guarded by an image of Ganesh, and murals of the Garuda bird and the monkey-god Hanuman decorate the doorway. Founded in the early 15th century, it houses an image of Mahalakshmi, the great goddess, spirited away from the Portuguese in 1565 (*see* www.mahalaxmidev.com).

Shri Mahalsa Temple ★★

This temple, close to **Mardol** village on the main Ponda–Old Goa road, dates from the 17th century and is noteworthy for the elaborately carved wooden pillars which support its roof. A 21-tiered brass column supporting a tiny effigy of the Garuda bird, the mount of Vishnu, stands in the courtyard, overlooked by a pink and white pagoda-like tower. The temple is sacred to Mahalsa, an incarnation of the goddess Lakshmi.

Shri Mangesh Temple ★★★

This temple at **Priol**, 8km (5 miles) north of Ponda town, is Goa's most impressive Hindu temple, and if you have the time or inclination to visit only one, this should be it. A pagoda-like octagonal lamp tower, the tallest and most impressive in the state, rises above a pretty, recently restored main building in the typically Goan colours of primrose yellow, white and terracotta. The temple is built around the largest water tank in Goa and is surrounded by greenery and palm trees. Mangesh is a benevolent aspect of Shiva. The temple dates from the 17th–18th centuries (*see* www.shrimangesh.org).

Ganesh temple ★

This small temple at **Candola** village, some 24km (15 miles) from Ponda on the banks of the Mandovi River, is dedicated to the elephant-headed god of prosperity and wisdom, Ganesh. Ganesh or Ganapati was the protective god of Ela, the earlier Hindu city on the site of Old Goa, and the older of the two Ganesh statues in this shrine was removed from there after the city fell to Muslim invaders from Bijapur.

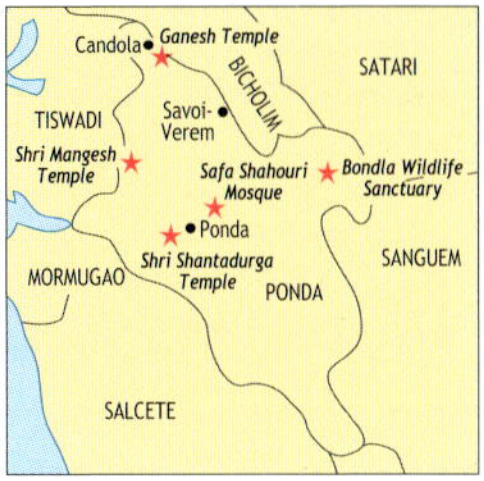

Anand Dewasthan Temple ★

The Anand Dewasthan Temple, near **Savoi-Verem** village, features on a number of tour itineraries but is perhaps less striking than some of the other shrines of Ponda province, having no multi-tiered tower or domed roof. It is, however, prettily located in the countryside near the upper Mandovi river.

▼ *Below: The Shri Mangesh temple is one of the most enchanting temples in Goa.*

Lingam

Lingam (the singular is linga) are phallic stone fertility symbols, representing the Hindu god Shiva in his reproductive role. Mukhalingam are a variant on the theme, in which a stylized face is carved on the head of the linga.

Safa Shahouri Mosque (Masjid) ★★★

Just outside Ponda, the mosque was built at the command of **Ali Adil Shah**, Sultan of Bijapur, in 1560. It was partially destroyed by the Portuguese, and is one of only two mosques surviving from the Bijapur period. Compared with the nearby Hindu temples, it is a plain, restrained building with Bijapuri-style pointed arches inside and out. The stumps of octagonal pillars that surround it indicate that the pitched roof originally extended to cover the stone platform around the *masjid*. Stone steps lead from the entrance to the large tank on the south side of the building.

Bondla Wildlife Sanctuary ★★

The smallest and most easily accessible of Goa's three wildlife sanctuaries is around 20km (12½ miles) east of Ponda town and is featured on a number of tour itineraries. Visitors expecting a safari-style experience or a trek through virgin forest will be disappointed, as Bondla is a pocket-sized park. Its main attraction is a series of zoo-style enclosures. Species on show include **leopard**, **sambar deer** and **gaur**. A walk in the beautifully landscaped grounds will also offer a

▶ *Right: Peacocks run wild in the grounds of the Bondla Wildlife Sanctuary.*

▲ *Above: The Tambdi Surla Temple near Molem.*

glimpse of the resident troop of wild **macaque monkeys**, a rarity in the more heavily populated areas of Goa. The sanctuary also has a small restaurant and half a dozen tourist bungalows, making it a pleasant place to stay overnight on a longer exploration of Ponda province. A short stop at Bondla is included on a number of excursions operated by the Goa Tourist Development Corporation.

SANGUEM AND SURROUNDS

There isn't an awful lot to do in the little town of Sanguem so it would be wise to pass it by and head for Sanguem province's three main attractions.

Tambdi Surla Temple (Shri Mahadeva Temple) ★★★

This temple is 8km (5 miles) from **Molem** village and 3km (2 miles) from the smaller village of **Surla**. There is a real thrill of discovery in the approach to the temple which stands aloof from Goa's more populated areas on the verge of the thickly wooded **Western Ghats**, which form a dramatic backdrop. Set in a riverside clearing and surrounded by tropical forest, this is the only surviving temple from the era of the Kadamba kings. Built between the 11th and 13th centuries,

Wildlife

Hunting, poaching and deforestation together with ever-increasing population pressure have placed India's wildlife in great difficulty. Larger species such as tiger, elephant, leopard and rhinoceros are now confined to the country's network of wildlife reserves, of which there are now currently more than 100.

Temple Etiquette

All of Goa's Hindu temples are in use as places of worship. To avoid giving offence, visitors should dress modestly (skimpy beachwear is unacceptable). Footwear must be removed before entering the temple precincts so take a shoulder bag to deposit your shoes in. Many temples have a prominently placed collection box and a small donation will always be appreciated.

it looks far more satisfyingly ancient than the often modernized, European influenced temples found around Ponda.

The temple has two halls and an inner sanctuary, all standing on a raised plinth, with flights of steps leading to entrances on the north, south and east sides of the main hall. The plain exterior is decorated with stylized rosette reliefs. The ***shikhara*** (spire), now truncated, rises in three massive stone tiers above the sanctuary and displays remarkable carvings of Brahma, Shiva and Parvati. The temple is built of black basalt, which was preferred by Kadamba masons because it could be carved more cleanly and lasted far longer than the soft, crumbly laterite which is the only stone found in Goa. Importing the necessary stone, probably from Karnataka, must have been a considerable challenge. Ten plain pillars support the roof of the main hall, with four elaborately carved columns in the middle of the hall. The rear walls display niches for now-missing statues.

Rivona Caves ★

About 5km (3 miles) from Sanguem town, a series of artificial caves carved in the rock were originally a **Buddhist monastery**. Built around the 7th century AD, the caves were later taken over as Hindu shrines. These caves resemble mine shafts and one in particular is guarded by a worn 16th-century image of the ever-popular monkey-god **Hanuman**. The Hindu shrines don't really justify a special journey, but are worth making the relatively short detour on the way to the more striking Tambdi Surla temple near Molem village.

Bhagwan Mahavir Wildlife Sanctuary ★★

This wildlife reserve is much larger than that at Bondla, covering 240km² (96 sq miles) of forested hills to the east of **Molem** village, in a prominent strip of territory jutting east towards the Karnataka border. It provides a refuge for Indian wildlife, including a large herd of **gaur**, **Indian elephant**, **leopard**, **black panther** and several species of **deer**. **Tigers** are reportedly sometimes seen by rangers, but are very rare and are always under threat from poachers.

Much of the reserve is covered by thick forest and the network of hiking trails and four-wheel-drive tracks is still incomplete. Eventually, it is planned to build a number of night hides with salt licks to attract larger, shyer animals. Most of the larger game animals keep to the trackless southern section, and at present are rarely spotted by visitors.

The park does, however, offer superb **birdwatching**, with virtually all the main south Indian species represented, and plenty of clear views over the lower, rolling grassland section of the park where gaur are sometimes seen as well as macaque and other common Indian monkeys.

The Goa Tourist Development Corporation operates a small number of rooms in tourist bungalows which are close to the main gate of the sanctuary, and an overnight stay allows you to join one of the morning and evening game drives. These drives offer the best chance of seeing game such as gaur, deer and, with luck, elephant.

◀ *Left: A macaque monkey in the forests of Bhagwan Mahavir Wildlife Sanctuary.*

Dudhsagar Falls ★★★

The rail journey from Vasco da Gama or Margao to Dudhsagar Falls in Goa's western mountain ranges effectively gives the visitor a bargain-priced tour of the state. Departing from the station at Vasco not long after dawn, the train trundles through the countryside of coastal Mormugao and Salcete provinces to reach **Margao**, the largest town in southern Goa, about an hour later. Travellers from the south Goa coast resorts can join the train here. As the line winds eastward from Margao the countryside changes, and at **Calem**, where the hills begin, a second engine is attached to push the train up the steepest stretch of track to the station at **Castle Rock**.

There are fine views back over the lowlands of Goa and along the vista of the Western Ghats as the train switch-backs through the hills, eventually arriving at Dudhsagar halt within sight of the falls high above and to the right of the track. The station shelter is at 241m (783ft) above sea level, but the falls start high above and plummet 600m (1950ft) to the foam-white pools below.

▼ *Below: The railway line to Karnataka passes Dudhsagar Falls, the highest in India.*

The falls are formed by the **Candepar River**, and are at their best in September, just after the end of the monsoon season, when they are at their fullest.

A path leads from the railway to the lower pool, where you can swim. The walk down is relatively easy but the 150m (500ft) zigzag ascent is taxing.

Unfortunately there are no refreshments at the falls or at the railway halt so bring a picnic and cold drinks from your hotel.

Best Times to Visit

The best time of the year to visit is from **mid-Sept** to **mid-Feb** when daytime temperatures average around 27°C (80°F).

Getting There

To get to **Ponda** there are several daily **buses** from Panaji (1½ hours) and Margao (1 hour). To **Sanguem** town you can take several daily buses from Margao (1½ hours). There are several **trains** daily from Vasco da Gama (3 hours) and Margao (2 hours) to **Dudhsagar Falls** which will take you directly to below the falls. You can also catch this train at Candolim or Dabolim, which may be more convenient if you're staying at one of the nearby south coast resorts. To get to the **Bhagwan Mahavir Wildlife Sanctuary**, catch the Dudhsagar train as far as Colem railway station, 3km (2 miles) from Molem village at the gateway to the park and then hire an **auto-rickshaw** or **motorbike** to the park entrance office.

Getting Around

The easiest way to explore Ponda and Sanguem is to rent a **car** with a driver from your resort or in Panaji, or to go on one of the organized tours (*see* Tours and Excursions). Public transport other than the **bus** and **train** is thin on the ground and you are unlikely to find even local yellow-topped **taxis**.

Where to Stay

Accommodation in Eastern Goa is limited, but the range is expanding. The Goa Tourism Development Corporation (www.goa-tourism.com) operates bungalow accommodation at the Bondla and Bhagwan Mahavir wildlife sanctuaries; these offer restaurants with basic menus.

Dudhsagar Spa Resort, Dudhsagar, tel: 0832 261 2238, www.goa-tourism.com This village-style resort offers accommodation in air-conditioned rooms, cottages and luxury tents in leafy gardens. Its restaurant is one of the few places to eat near Dudhsagar Falls.

Farmagudi Hill Resort, Old Goa Highway, Farmagudi, tel: 08322 335 122, www.goa-tourism.com Near Safa Masjid and Ponda Temples, this hotel has 39 rooms including air-conditioned suites.

Where to Eat

This is the least touristy part of Goa and there are no restaurants catering specifically for foreign visitors. Eating places tend to be extremely simple and English is not widely spoken. If you are travelling on an organized tour a snack lunch and refreshments will probably be provided (though it is always best to check). If you are travelling by rail you can buy snacks and cold drinks from **vendors** at every station, or take a pre-packed **picnic**. Most resort hotels and many restaurants are happy to provide this. The stainless-steel tiffin cans with wire handles sold in local stores and markets are an excellent way of carrying picnic meals. There are GTDC-run **restaurants** at both wildlife sanctuaries, but the menu is more limited than it would be at one of the beach resorts.

Tours and Excursions

Daily tours of the temples are available from Panaji and main south coast resorts. Information and bookings from the GTDC or **Goa Tourist Development Corporation** (www.goa-tourism.com).

Sahakari Spice Farm, Ponda-Belgaum Highway, Curti, tel: 0832 231 2394, www.sahakarifarms.com Visit an authentic spice plantation which also has the best restaurant in this part of Goa.

Goa Rafting (tel: 0738 723 8866, www.goarafting.com) operates white-water trips on the Tilari River, on the border between Goa and Karnataka.

Useful Contacts

There are no tourist or information offices outside Panaji; for information *see* p.55, Panaji and Central Goa at a Glance.

EASTERN GOA	J	F	M	A	M	J	J	A	S	O	N	D
AVERAGE TEMP. °C	25	26	27	29	30	28	26	26	26	27	27	27
AVERAGE TEMP. °F	76	77	78	84	85	84	77	77	77	78	78	78
DAYS OF RAINFALL	1	0	1	8	9	30	30	30	20	10	5	5
RAINFALL mm	2	0	4	17	18	500	890	340	277	122	20	30
RAINFALL in	-	-	.15	.9	.9	20	36	14	11	5	.1	1.2

6
Southern Goa

Southern Goa has become increasingly popular since the flood of charter flights begun in the 1980s. Its beaches are the equal of any in the north, and despite the tourism boom are still generally less crowded. They also have the added advantage that, since there are no major rivers between the southern provinces and the airport at Dabolim, coach transfer times are much shorter.

Salcete province in the north borders Mormugao and is separated from Ponda by the upper Zuari River. **Quepem**, the next province south, is sandwiched between Salcete and Goa's southernmost province, **Canacona**. Salcete's coastline is a 20km (12½ miles) stretch of continuous sand which extends unbroken from **Cansaulim** to the mouth of the **Sal River** in the south. Cansaulim is administratively part of Mormugao province but as it is part of this southern beach strip it is included in this chapter.

Quepem, which has only a tiny section of seacoast between the mouth of the Sal River and the promontory of **Cabo de Rama** (Cape Rama), has all but escaped tourist attention and has no outstanding sightseeing attractions.

Canacona has until recently been the south's equivalent of Pernem province in the north: a last escape for those who are prepared to accept the simplest of food and accommodation in order to find the perfect beach and escape the tourism boom. Its relative inaccessibility has given it considerable immunity from development until now but with the construction of the **Konkan** railway line its days of glorious isolation are numbered.

Don't Miss

*** **Loutolim:** south Goa's prettiest traditional village.
*** **Colva:** the finest beach in Goa.
*** **Palolem:** last chance to see this unspoiled beach before development takes it over completely.
** **Chandrapura:** fascinating archaeological site.

◀ *Opposite: Colva Beach offers spectacular sunsets over the Arabian Sea.*

MARGAO (MADGAON) AND SURROUNDS

Margao, the capital of **Salcete** province, is a sleepy market town and road-rail junction which only seems to wake up fully when its sprawling covered market is in full swing. Margao is first and foremost a farming town, and most foreigners pause here only to change buses on the way to or from the Salcete coast resorts, or perhaps to visit the market. Like Panaji, the town clearly displays its Portuguese heritage, especially in the town centre streets between **Jorge Barreto Park** and **Church Square**, which are lined by faded 18th- and 19th-century mansions.

Church of the Holy Spirit ★

The 17th-century Church of the Holy Spirit, built soon after the Portuguese conquest of Salcete, occupies one side of a square of once-grand colonial buildings. In the centre of the **Church Square** stands an ornate, whitewashed monumental cross which is all that remains of the earlier, 16th-century church, destroyed in a Muslim attack only 14 years after its foundation in 1565. The present church dates from 1675 and has a florid, highly ornamented baroque façade. To enter the church, walk through the archway on the south side. This leads to a courtyard which has been created by the surrounding clerical buildings. Notice the beautifully carved Indian Baroque altarpieces and the highly detailed sanctuary.

Ancestral Goa

This purpose-built visitor attraction at Loutolim features a bird habitat, spice gardens, art gallery and handicraft centre, as well as a 250-year-old Goan mansion, and 'Mini Goa', an exhibition of regional culture and tradition. It has its own restaurant. Open daily, 09:00–17:00, tel: 0832 277 7044.

Rachol Fort and Seminary ★★

The seminary was transferred in 1580 from Margao, which had been repeatedly attacked by the Muslims, to the greater security of the fort at Rachol. Dating from the 14th century, the fort was conquered by the **Raja of Vijayanagar** in 1520, and shortly afterwards ceded to his Portuguese allies, who turned it into their strongest inland fortification. By the mid-19th century, however, the threat of invasion by Muslim or Hindu neighbours was over, and the Portuguese decommissioned the fort and allowed its ramparts to crumble. There is now little left of the outer walls, which may have been quarried for stone to build the Rachol Seminary. This Catholic college became Goa's leading centre of learning and is still in service. Its dignified, dazzlingly white outer walls conceal a broad inner courtyard painted in a rather festive shade of pink. The enormous façade of the seminary church, which is similar within to Bom Jesus in Old Goa, occupies one entire side of the courtyard of the old college. The seminary produces what is reputedly Goa's best feni liquor.

▲ *Above: Stucco-fronted houses, typical of the Portuguese colonial period, line the sleepy streets of Margao.*

Loutolim ★★★

North of Margao is Loutolim, a strong contender for the title of prettiest village in Goa, with many delightfully attractive and well-preserved homes dating back to the heyday of the Portuguese empire. On a bright day, Loutolim can be blinding, with the sun blazing back from every whitewashed wall, highlighted by typically Goan touches of ochre and pink. The village radiates from a central square, overlooked by a delightful parish church, having a façade that is a fantasy of Baroque columns and arches.

Maratha Wars

Portugal came closest to losing its Indian territories in their war with the Marathas of Maharashtra (1737–39). After capturing many of Portugal's northern strongholds, these fierce Hindu warriors swept into Goa itself, capturing Margao and threatening the capital. The Portuguese defence, however, was so stubborn that the Marathas agreed to a peace treaty in May 1739, though Portugal lost much territory in the north.

▲ *Above: Goan villagers traditionally don brightly dyed new clothing for the many Hindu and Christian festivals which punctuate the year.*

Chandor ★

The village of Chandor is 5km (3 miles) from Margao and is the site of one of Goa's colourful festivals, the **Fair of Reis Magos** (the Magi Kings or Three Wise Men), on 6 January each year. The village's central square is dominated by the vast arched frontage of one of the grand aristocratic homes which are characteristic of Salcete province. The **Menezes Braganza House** is open to the public and offers a fascinating glimpse of how wealthy Goan families lived in the 18th and 19th centuries, when the major part of this house was built. The Menezes Braganza family, early converts to the Roman Catholic faith, have lived here since the 16th century. The marble-floored grand salon, the large library, the banqueting hall, and private chapel are all indications of the family's considerable wealth and status.

Chandrapura ★

The earliest ancient settlement to be discovered in Goa lies 2km (1¼ miles) from Chandor. The site of Chandrapura first drew the attention of archaeologists in 1929, and excavations since then indicate that the **ancient fortress** and **temple** found here date back to the 3rd century BC. In the late 6th century, this river port became the capital of the region under the **Kadamba** dynasty. In 1052 they moved their capital to Govalpuri between the Zuari and Mandovi rivers – the exact site is not known. Considerable imagination is needed to picture the substantial city which once stood here, as all that remains are the stone foundations of the fortress and the brick walls of a temple to **Shiva** which stood within.

Dhobi

The Indian *dhobi* (laundry) system never fails to astonish first-time visitors. In a country where many services – such as hotel and airline reservations, telephones and every aspect of government bureaucracy – work slowly and unreliably if at all, the *dhobi walla* (laundry man) is a shining example of superbly efficient service at a very low price. Nowhere else in the world can you get your clothes washed so quickly, cheaply and efficiently – and all by hand.

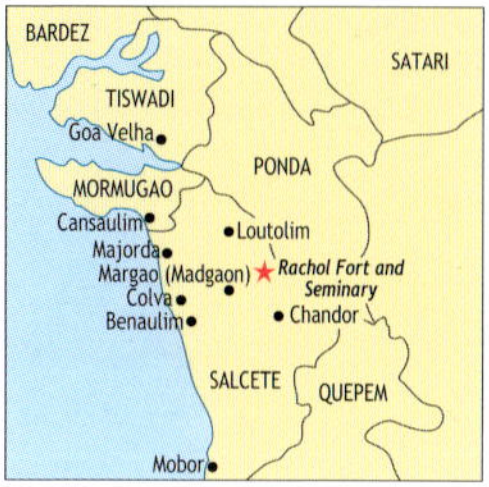

SOUTHERN BEACH VILLAGES

Goa's longest beach – and one of the finest in Asia – starts just south of the **Bogmalo** headland in Mormugao province and seems to go on almost forever. Hotels and small resorts are scattered along its 25km (15 mile) length, clustering around former fishing villages. Most of them are set several hundred metres back from the beach for protection from the powerful waves which lash and clean the beach during the summer monsoon. A coastal highway runs parallel to the shore as far as the **Sal** estuary, connecting this string of villages. The Konkan railway line runs through southern Salcete province to Margao, connecting this part of Goa to points south. Predictably, tourism development is gradually filling the gaps between villages but there are still long stretches of near-deserted sand between the little clusters of restaurants and guesthouses.

Cashews

Brought to India by the Portuguese, the cashew trees which cover much of inland Goa are one of Goa's biggest export earners. Roasted cashews, which are sold loose in bulk in most markets, are a good buy to take home. Cashews are also made into *feni*, which is distilled from juice pressed from the bright yellow fruit.

◀ *Left: Tourist money attracts troops of young beach vendors to drive a hard bargain on Benaulim beach.*

▲ *Above: Slender palm trees line the high watermark along the majestic sweep of Colva beach.*

Coconuts

The coconut palms which line Goa's coast are more than just decorative. Together with cashew trees, coconut palms occupy about half the state's farmland, providing food, drink, and cash crop. Dried coconut meat is exported, as is coir, the rough fibre made from the coconut husk. Discarded shells may be used as fuel. Beach hawkers make a living selling delicious drinking coconuts to sunbathers on holiday beaches. Toddy or *arrack*, the fermented sap of the palm tree, makes quite an intoxicating drink! Even more potent is coconut *feni*, the spirit distilled from *arrack*.

Cansaulim ★★

Not to be confused with Candolim in Bardez province, this village marks the northern beginning of south Goa's fabulous beach strip. From here the beach blends seamlessly with Colva, and the sands then run unbroken as far as the Sal River. Because of its proximity to **Dabolim Airport**, which is accessible by road and rail, Cansaulim is amongst the busiest of the small southern Goan resorts, but still far quieter than the more popular resorts of northern Goa.

Majorda ★★

Majorda is situated 5km (3 miles) south of Cansaulim and set some 2km (1¼ miles) inland from the beach. Majorda also has a railway station, making it easily accessible. Like Cansaulim, its beach is its main attraction, but a late 18th-century **Church of Our Lady** lends the village some historic interest.

Colva ★★★

Colva village, midway along the stretch of beach which bears its name, is about 8km (5 miles) west of **Margao**, the provincial capital. Set about 1.5km (1 mile) inland from the beach, it has grown into the biggest village on the southern coast and is the hub of a string of hotels and restaurants,

spreading to north and south along the beach. Though the village has already come a long way since the 1960s when it was little more than a fishing settlement and favoured by low-budget independent travellers, it is still far from being overdeveloped by international resort standards. Most of the hotels are fairly small, and much of the accommodation available still caters for the less well-heeled traveller as well as to mid-market package holiday-makers. In fact, most of the development is driven by the Indian domestic tourism market and Colva is far from being overwhelmed by the international package holiday business. Canoe-like fishing boats no longer line the beach, as most of the local fishermen have invested in sturdier wooden tubs that bob at anchor just offshore.
A church of **Our Lady of Mercy** stands at the village cross-roads. Typically brilliant white on the exterior, it has a gaudy ornately decorated interior. Founded in 1630, the church was rebuilt by the Jesuit order during the 18th century.

Kites

The buzzard-like, carrion-eating kites are frequently seen circling above villages and fields. Most common around towns and villages is the **pariah kite** with dark brown plumage and a prominent forked tail. Along the coast and around lakes and rivers look out for the slightly smaller **Brahminy kite**, with a rounded tail, chestnut wings and black and white head and breast.

◀ *Left: Water buffalo are used to plough Goa's green and gold rice fields.*

Kingfishers

The most commonly seen of India's many colourful kingfishers are the **lesser pied kingfisher** with its speckled black and white plumage and the **white-breasted kingfisher**, recognizable by its turquoise wings, chestnut front and head and white breast and throat. Both species can be seen perching on telephone wires or branches by streams, ponds and flooded fields, or hovering above the water.

Benaulim ★★★

Benaulim village, immediately south of Colva, is landmarked by the hilltop church of **St John the Baptist** which stands above the village about 1km (2/3 mile) inland from the beach. This is the quietest section of the southern coast with few hotels of any size, and remains a favourite with independent travellers. Further south, small guesthouses and beach restaurants are dotted along the sections of beach close to the inland villages of **Varca** and **Cavelossim**.

Mobor ★★

Mobor village stands on the narrow northern headland at the mouth of the **Sal River**, marking the southern end of the Salcete province beach strip. Despite its relative remoteness, this is the most upmarket resort in southern Goa, with a clutch of expensive, top-notch hotels set in immaculately manicured grounds. Unless you are staying in one of these resort complexes, however, Mobor does not offer much to see or do. There are virtually no facilities for visitors in Mobor village and it remains little more than a ramshackle fishing hamlet. Keen birders, though, will find the Sal River estuary attracts many species of seabirds and waterfowl, including huge flocks of gulls and several species of kingfisher, stork and heron.

Betul ★★

Quepem province is almost landlocked, with only a short stretch of coast between the Sal estuary and the provincial border with Canacona province to the south. Betul is the province's only beach settlement. Getting to this settlement, on the south shore of the Sal estuary, entails a detour inland to the footbridge or ferry crossing. The visitor in search of the impossible dream of an as-yet-untouched Goan beach will find the journey well worthwhile. The minor inconvenience of crossing the river has saved Betul from tourism, at least for the time being, and it is very much a village for travellers seeking a perfect beach and the simplest of food and accommodation. Unlike most of the Goan fishing settlements, Betul

◀ *Left: Beach umbrellas at peaceful Mobor are a sign of increasing tourism encroachment.*

is built close to the high-tide line as the Sal headland protects it from the worst of the monsoon gales. It is also within easy reach of the equally fine, peaceful beaches of Canacona province next door, from which it is separated by the rocky headland of **Cabo de Rama**.

CANACONA

Goa's most southerly province, bordered by Karnataka state to the south, is its quietest and least developed. Until recently, its superb, untouched beaches and tiny fishing villages attracted only the most determined of travellers: those who were prepared to accept a very basic standard of living, use uncomfortable local public transport, and dispense with all the tourist trimmings. The opening of the **Konkan** railway, connecting the province with Margao and the 21st century, is set to change everything, though perhaps not overnight.

In the meantime, Canacona's **beaches** – a series of crescent-shaped sweeps of sand separated by headlands and backed by hills – remain idyllic. Its hilly hinterland, much of which is given over to the **Cotigao Wildlife Sanctuary**, is one of Goa's great escapes and is dramatically different from the pastoral scenes of the central provinces. It was among the last segments of present-day Goa to be added to the Portuguese colony, being taken over by treaty from the **King of Sunda** in 1791.

Egrets

These white-plumed relatives of the heron are seen everywhere in paddy fields and among cattle. The **cattle egret** is the most common, tall and recognizable by its orange upper plumage in the breeding season and by its yellow beak and legs. It feeds in cattle fields, often perching on the animals' backs, and in village trash heaps. Similar but slightly larger is the **little egret**, which has a black beak and legs and stalks its prey in shallow water. Also seen in ponds, lakes and flooded fields is the **large egret**, with a yellow beak and black legs.

Chaudi is Canacona province's administrative centre and transport hub, but has no facilities for visitors and no sights to visit. It's really no more than a place to change buses. Since the late 1990s, it has been the province's main station on the Konkan railway line, and this is bringing gradual change to many villages along the new track.

Rollers and Bee-eaters

Among the most colourful birds of the Indian countryside, the **roller** has a turquoise-green back and wings, a deep blue tail and a pinkish breast, with purple touches on the neck and nape. It is seen either perching on wires or branches in open country, or in distinctive gliding, swooping flight. The related green **bee-eater** is even more vivid, with bright green plumage, blue chin and throat, and a yellowish head.

Cabo de Rama ★

Cabo de Rama (Cape Rama) juts into the Arabian Sea close to Canacona's border with Quepem province. Its strategic advantages were obvious from the earliest times, and according to local legend the warrior-god **Rama** took refuge here after being defeated by his demonic enemies. In historic times, the site attracted the attention first of the local rulers and then of the Portuguese, who seized the fort from the **King of Sunda** in 1763. They were responsible for adding a small chapel – which can still be seen inside the ramparts –

and substantial barrack buildings, which have crumbled into a maze of roofless walls. A deep ditch was the first line of defence and is overlooked by massive, crumbling walls and the tumbledown remains of the main gate. The stronghold has been disused since the 1830s, when the Portuguese abandoned it.

Palolem ★★

Some people think Palolem is the best beach in Goa. It is certainly one of the most visually appealing. A 1.5km (1 mile) curve of glowing gold sand is hemmed in by thickly wooded headlands. Offshore is a tiny islet which you can walk to at low tide. Coconut palms and a clutter of tiny, brightly painted beach bars line the top of the beach. Palolem village is little more than a line of shops, homes, and very simple restaurants either side of the road which connects the coast with Chaudi, the provincial capital.

◀ Opposite: Palm trees fringe a magnificent sunset at Palolem, one of Goa's remotest beach villages.
▼ Below: The long-tailed macaque monkey may be found in the Cotigao Wildlife sanctuary.

Cotigao Wildlife Sanctuary ★

Cotigao Wildlife Sanctuary is a 100km^2 (40-sq-mile) slice of hilly, forested land in the low foothills of the **Western Ghats** mountain range. It is most certainly the wildest of Goa's three wildlife sanctuaries, but is not very user-friendly. In order to explore it properly you must bring your own vehicle (preferably four-wheel-drive as there is only one dirt track within the sanctuary) or the area can be explored on foot. There are no food or lodging facilities.

SOUTHERN GOA AT A GLANCE

Best Times to Visit

As with other parts of Goa, **mid-September** to **mid-February** is the most favourable time to visit because the daytime temperatures average around 27°C (80°F).

Getting There

There are several daily **buses** to Margao from Panaji (2 hours) and Vasco da Gama (1 hour, 30 mins). Several daily **trains** (1 hour, 30 mins) arrive in Margao from Vasco da Gama. **Trains** travelling between Vasco da Gama and Margao also stop at Cansaulim and Majorda stations (about 25 mins and 35 mins respectively) for the southern beach villages. The **Konkan Railway** services run from Vasco and points to the north and onward to Ernakulam, also calling at Margao. **Buses** from Vasco to Cansaulim take around 45 minutes and buses to Majorda take approximately 55 minutes. There are several buses that run daily from Margao to Colva and Benaulim (15 mins) and to Mobor (30 mins). If you are heading for Betul, take the Mobor bus and cross the Sal River by the ferry or footbridge at the end of the paved road. There are several buses daily from Margao (1 hour) to Chaudi in Canacona as well as the rail service to Margao on the Konkan line. Getting to the fort at Cabo de Rama and the tiny neighbouring village involves either renting your own transport or a long walk from the nearest main road between Betul and Chaudi. Two buses daily leave from Chaudi for Palolem (30 mins). **Bicycles**, small **motorcycles** and **taxis** can be hired from the larger Colva beach resorts.

Getting Around

One of the best ways to explore the full length of the south coast beach strip is by motorcycle. Elsewhere, public transport is limited to **buses**.

Where to Stay

Most of the top international-brand hotels in Goa cluster around Majorda and Varca, and there are plenty of mid-range hotels here and at Colva.

Salcete

Luxury

The Leela, Goa, Mobor, Cavelossim, tel: 0832 662 1234, www.theleela.com The best beach resort in Goa and India. It has a huge, uncrowded beach, 18.2ha (45 acres) of landscaped grounds, lagoons, and a nine-hole golf course.

Majorda Beach Resort, Majorda, tel: 08322 88 1111, www.majordabeachresort.com Luxury 63-room resort; 10 self-contained villas.

Park Hyatt Goa Resort and Spa, tel: 08322 721 234, www.goa.park.hyatt.com World-class resort and spa on 45 beachfront acres at Arossim.

Alila Diwa Goa, Adao Wada, Majorda tel: 0832 274 6800, www.alilahotels.com Luxury resort and spa with 35 rooms, set among paddy fields close to the beach.

Mid-range

Casa Susegad, Orgao, Loutolim, tel: 0832 669 4444, www.casasusegad.com Colourful, luxurious boutique hotel in one of Goa's prettiest villages.

Heritage Village Club, Arossim Beach, Cansaulim, tel: 0832 699 4444, www.selecthotels.co.in Goa's first all-inclusive boutique resort, with five bars and restaurants, pool, and a range of sports, activities and entertainment.

Dona Sylvia Beach Resort, Cavelossim, tel: 08322 871 888, www.donasylvia.com Low-rise village-style resort; 174 rooms in Mediterranean-style bungalows, set in attractive grounds.

Budget

Casa de Morgado, Sontrant, Cortalim, tel: 08322 550 216, fax: 586 923, www.casademorgadogoa.com Family-run guesthouse in part of the region's architectural heritage – a 400-year-old house set among rice fields. Rooms have modern bathrooms and meals are lovingly prepared.

Betul

Mayfair Hideaway Spa

Resort, tel: 0958 293 9225, www.mayfairhotels.com The Betul area's first luxury hotel, with pool and landscaped gardens.

Canacona

Palolem has a handful of small guesthouses to complement the very basic camp site among trees near the beach.

Budget

Tito's Cafe del Mar, Palolem, tel: 0823 928 408, www.titosgroup.com Cafe-restaurant with air-conditioned and non-AC beach huts.

Palolem Guest House, Ourem, Palolem, tel: 08322 644 879, www.palolemguesthouse.com Posh by Palolem standards, with 25 en-suite air-conditioned rooms and restaurant-bar on south side of Palolem beach. Airport transfers available.

Bhakti Kutir, Palolem, Canacona, tel: 08322 643 469, www.bhaktikutir.com Funky collection of thatched bamboo cabins with en-suite 'bucket' bathrooms at the south end of Palolem beach. Every effort is made to keep the place eco-friendly, from organic, home-grown fruit and vegetables to biodegradable toilets.

Where to Eat

Salcete Beach villages

There are far too many beach shacks, bars and café-restaurants along this whole stretch of beach to list them all individually, and as the scene is constantly changing – with new places springing up and old places changing hands or changing their names – any attempt to do so or to single out individual places can only be misleading. Most have a similar bill of fare, on which seafood figures prominently. Most places to eat and drink are on or close to the beach, not in the villages which are set inland from the beach.

Be warned that during the early June to early September monsoon season, almost all of these close down, as well as many hotels and guesthouses that depend on the package holiday trade.

The main concentrations of places to eat outside the large resort hotels are at Cansaulim, Majorda, Colva, and Benaulim.

Mid-range

Fisherman's Wharf, Riverside, Salcete, tel: 09011 018866. Great location overlooking the Sal River.

Budget

Jazz Inn, Haathi Mahal Road, Cavelossim, tel: 0942 243 7682, www.jazzinngoa.in Good seafood, including kingfish, crab, prawns and lobster, and Goan dishes such as sorpotel and vindaloo.

Blue Whale Beach Shack, Bamboo House Resort, Mobor Beach. One of the best of Mobor's beach shacks, very affordable.

Tours and Excursions

Most of the larger hotels in Colva and other resorts offer tours and excursions to **Old Goa**, **Ponda**, the **Dudhsagar Falls** and other favourites.

At Mobor, Jack's Cruises (c/o Johnny Cool Restaurant, tel: 08322 871 132, www.jacksplacegoa.com) runs sunset and river cruises, fishing, dolphin-spotting trips, bird trekking and visits to the 'eagle bat' (flying fox) rookery up the Sal River. Others offer similar cruises – check the noticeboards outside the beach shack restaurants.

Useful Contacts

Tourist Information Office, Margao Residency, Railway Station Road, tel: 08322 715 204, fax: 720 470.

Goa Tourist Development Corporation, Patto, Panaji, operates accommodation and tours in Goa, tel: 08322 438 750, www.goa-tourism.com

SOUTHERN GOA	J	F	M	A	M	J	J	A	S	O	N	D
AVERAGE TEMP. °C	25	26	27	29	30	28	26	26	26	27	27	27
AVERAGE TEMP. °F	76	77	78	84	85	84	77	77	77	78	78	78
DAYS OF RAINFALL	1	0	1	8	9	30	30	30	20	10	5	5
RAINFALL mm	2	0	4	17	18	500	890	340	277	122	20	30
RAINFALL in	-	-	.15	.9	.9	20	36	14	11	5	.1	1.2

7
Karnataka and Kerala

It has been claimed that Goa, with its Portuguese colonial heritage, is the least Indian of India's many states. If this is the case, the regions around it will perhaps bear a closer resemblance to the India many visitors imagine: **Karnataka**, with its splendid palaces from the great days of the Muslim princes and magnificent temples; **Kerala**, with its fine beaches and vast stretches of inland waterways; and the vast state of **Maharashtra**, heartland of the great Mahratha empire. Each of these destinations offers a taste of a very different India; each has its own language, customs and costume, and a journey onward from Goa can be far more satisfying than a simple beach-based holiday.

Until recently, adding a trip to one of these neighbouring destinations onto a holiday in Goa posed quite a few problems. Overland travel tends to be time-consuming. The rail journey from Goa to **Bengaluru** (formerly known as **Bangalore**) in eastern Karnataka, for example, takes almost 24 hours and until recently air travel was unreliable as flights were very often overbooked or even cancelled. In recent years there has, however, been a vast improvement in regional air services, and flights from Goa to destinations in Karnataka and Kerala are now much more reliable and competitively priced. In addition, Kerala has become a holiday haven in its own right (and a competitor to Goa) with direct charter flights from European cities arriving in the favoured southern resort of **Trivandrum** in the winter months, which has the feel of an overgrown village despite its size.

Don't Miss

*** **Hampi:** ruined 14th-century city with many Hindu temples and palaces.
*** **Bijapur:** former capital of the great 15th-century Muslim empire of Bijapur.
*** **Aihole, Pattadakal and Badami:** treasuries of Hindu temple architecture dating from the 5th, 6th and 7th centuries.
** **Bengaluru:** Karnataka's cosmopolitan big city.
** **Mysore:** historic city with a rich royal heritage.

◀ *Opposite: The magnificent palace of the Maharajahs of Mysore.*

KARNATAKA AND KERALA

KARNATAKA

Karnataka, which borders Goa to the south and east, is a vast state which covers just over 190,000km² (73,340 sq miles) and is home to almost 45 million people. The most widely spoken language is **Kannada**. Much of the state is rolling plateau country, cut off from the coast by the steep ranges of the **Western Ghats**. The state has its own little-developed beaches but these are not very easy to get to and offer none of the facilities of the Goan and Keralan coasts. For the visitor travelling onward from Goa, Karnataka's main attractions are the historic cities and ruined temples and fortresses scattered throughout the region.

Among the most interesting sights in northern Karnataka are the relics of the **kingdoms of Muslim Bijapur** and **Hindu Vijayanagar**, whose rulers vied for control of Goa over several centuries. **Mysore**, in the southern part of the state, is also well worth a visit.

The contrasts between traditional and modern India are perhaps stronger here than anywhere else in the south. In rural villages the ox-drawn plough and cart are still the norm and farming is still labour intensive. However, **Bengaluru**, the state capital, is the proud centre of India's space programme and a computer industry which exports millions of dollars' worth of sophisticated software via satellite to customers in Asia, Europe and the United States of America, earning the region the nickname 'Silicon Plateau'.

Karnataka is also quite a way off the most heavily travelled tourist routes, and visitors arriving from the more frequently visited cities of northern India will find very little of the high-pressure touting which surrounds the country's more popular sightseeing destinations.

Hampi ★★

The ruined capital of the mighty 14th-century **Vijayanagar** empire is 13km (6 miles) from the modern town of **Hospet** and 330km (205 miles) northeast of Bengaluru. Now a UNESCO World Heritage Centre, it is the most striking of the region's ruined cities, landmarked by towering temple *ziggurats* (towers). Restoration of its superb collection of temples and palaces continues. Set against a backdrop of rugged, rocky hills, the city is surrounded on three sides by the **Tungabhadra River**. Remnants of its seven rings of ramparts can still be seen. Within them, the kings of Vijayanagar ruled their empire from a city of half a million people, defended by a mighty army. Founded in 1336, the empire reached its zenith in the early 16th century, when it controlled virtually all of southern India. The end came in 1565, when it was sacked by a Muslim army.

▼ *Below: A bearded* sadhu *(Hindu holy man) sounds a traditional conch shell trumpet to announce a Hindu feast day.*

Hampi's Sights

The oversized set of scales which stood at the **King's Balance** were used annually to weigh the king against the tribute of gold and precious stones brought to him, which was then donated to the city temples. Remnants of frescoes and carved friezes decorate the square stone tank known as the **Queen's Bath** which was once covered by a vaulted canopy. The **Lotus Mahal** is a two-storey building next to the Queen's Bath and is a pretty mixture of Muslim and Hindu influences. It housed the royal ladies-in-waiting.

Built on an appropriately vast scale, the 10 vaulted chambers of the **Elephant Stables** surround a central pavilion which housed the keepers of the royal elephants. The most glorious of the city's temples, the **Vittala Temple** is noted for its series of columns, each carved from a single piece of rock and each chiming a different note when struck. Other highlights include a stone temple chariot drawn by elephants. Still used by Hindu worshippers, the temple to **Virupaksha** (one of the aspects of Shiva) is the most prominent building on the site. Its two courtyards are dominated by a huge stone **gopuram** (gateway) some 50m (164 ft) in height. The 6.7m (22ft) monolith of **Ugra Narasimha** depicts Vishnu in his incarnation as Narasimha, the mythical half-lion, half-man.

▶ *Right: The massive temple chariot carved from stone is a highlight of Vithala.*

Bijapur ★

Bijapur, in northern Karnataka, 530km (331 miles) north of Bengaluru and 200km (125 miles) from Hampi, was the inland capital of the **Adil Shahi** dynasty who wrested Goa and much of the region from the control of **Vijayanagar** during the 15th century. Its treasury of graceful Islamic architecture, dating from the 16th and 17th centuries, is strikingly different from the massive temples of contemporary Hindu sites, and is equally impressive.

Bijapur's Sights

One of the world's largest unsupported domes, the Gol Gumbaz houses the tomb of **Mohammed Adil Shah III** (1626–56). Its remarkable acoustics carry the slightest sound across the vast interior space. **Jumma Masjid**, a glorious mosque, with its gleaming gold dome and slender minarets, is one of the finest in India. Built by the first Adil Shah (1557–80), its proudest possession is a gold-lettered copy of the Koran and gilt Koranic verses which decorate the interior.

Claimed to have inspired the Taj Mahal, the **Ibrahim Roza** was built by Ibrahim Adil Shah II (1580–1626) as a mausoleum for his wife, the Taj Sultana. **Malik-e-Maidan**, a vast bronze artillery piece, 4m (14ft) long and weighing more than 50 tons, was seized as a war trophy from the rival kings of Purandar. The name means 'ruler of the plains'.

Aihole, Pattadakal and Badami

These three superb temple towns – successively capitals of the Hindu Chalukya kings in the 5th, 6th and 7th centuries – lie within a 13km (8 mile) radius of one another. Located 125km (78 miles) north of Hampi and 75km (48 miles) south of Bijapur, they can be visited en route between the two.

Aihole, known as the 'cradle of Indian temple architecture', has 125 intricately carved Hindu temples. The oldest, the Lad Khan Temple, dates from the 5th century AD. **Pattadakal**, now a World Heritage Centre, has 10 fine temples, the most impressive being the vast **Virupaksha Temple**, dating from the 8th century. **Badami** is best known for four splendid

Bijapur History

The **Adil Shahi** dynasty who made Bijapur their capital from 1489 to 1686 emerged as rulers of the region when the earlier Muslim **Bahmani** kingdom disintegrated in 1482. They ruled a swathe of territory which included most of what is now Goa and much of northern Karnataka and southern Maharashtra. They lost Goa to the Portuguese in the early 16th century, and were conquered by the **Mughals** of Delhi in the late 17th century.

Space City

With an urban population estimated at just under 5.5 million in 2010, Bengaluru is now India's third largest city, nudging Kolkata into fourth place. Its prosperity and growth are mainly based on information technology. The hub of India's call-centre, computer and software industries, and ground base for the country's space programme, it is proud of its 'Silicon Plateau' nickname.

cave temples with walls adorned by huge carvings of Shiva, Vishnu and other gods. Opposite the cave temples is **Badami Archaeological Museum** (open 10:00–17:00, Saturday–Thursday), with stone sculptures and friezes from the Chaluka era (www.asi.nic.in).

BENGALURU

Founded by the Hindu ruler **Kempegowda** in 1537 and strengthened by the Muslim sultan **Hyder Ali** and his heir **Tipu Sultan**, Bengaluru is one of India's most modern cities. At 1000m (3250ft) above sea level, its clement climate made it a favourite with the British after their conquest of the region from Tipu in 1799. By urban Indian standards, it is strikingly green with several fine public parks and gardens and a cosmopolitan laid-back air which sets it apart from other south Indian cities.

Sultan's Palace **

Originally within the walls of the sultan's fort, the small two-storey palace with its arches and arcades was begun by **Hyder Ali** in 1778. His heir finished the work the following year. Open 06:00–18:00, daily, except on public holidays.

▼ *Below: The massive Government House is a relic of the British Raj.*

The Fort ★★

Massive stone bastions and ramparts mark the site of the stronghold, first of the 16th-century king **Kempegowda** and later of the 18th-century **Muslim** sultans. Open 08:00 to sunset, daily.

Bull Temple ★★

Bengaluru's oldest temple dates from **Kempegowda**'s 16th-century reign. The 4.6m (15ft) statue of the sacred bull **Nandi** is carved from a single block of granite.

Lal Bagh Gardens ★

The 100ha (240 acre) gardens were laid out by **Hyder Ali** in 1760 and enlarged by his son **Tipu Sultan**. They are among the finest public gardens in India.

Cubbon Park ★

The 121ha (300-acre) city-centre gardens were laid out in 1864 and named after the British Commissioner of Mysore state, Lieutenant General Sir Mark Cubbon (1784–1861). In the park is the **Karnataka Museum and Venkatappa Art Gallery**, open 10:00–1 7:00, Tuesday–Saturday (www.karnatakaarchaeology.gov.in).

Nrityagram Dance Village ★★

Some 30km (20 miles) outside Bengaluru is this unique village where young women from all over India come to learn ancient dance forms through *guru-shishya parampara*, the age-old system whereby the tradition, culture and values of centuries are transmitted by word of mouth from teacher (*guru*) to disciple (*shishya*). You can watch dancers at their lessons and take part in yoga and meditation classes (*see* www.nrityagram.org).

MYSORE

Mysore, 140km (90 miles) southwest of Bengaluru, is one of southern India's most appealing cities. Like Bengaluru, its climate is comparatively temperate, thanks to its location 770m (2526ft) above sea level. The Wodeyar maharajahs became rulers of the city and the surrounding region during the 14th century. They were driven out by **Hyder Ali** in 1759 but regained the city 40 years later after the overthrow of **Tipu Sultan** and his French allies by the British in 1799. The **Wodeyars** then became rulers of the entire state under British tutelage and remained so until Independence. The city owes most of its striking landmarks to its princely rulers.

Tipu Sultan

Tipu Sultan of Mysore was the last of the Indian rulers to resist the British. He was an astute politican as well as a competent general. Hiring European mercenaries to train his Muslim troops, he also allied himself with the French against the British in India. In 1799, commanded by **Lord Wellesley** (later the Duke of Wellington), the British invaded in force, and Tipu was killed in the battle for his fortress of **Seringapatam**.

Royal Palace ★★★

When the maharajah's palace was gutted by fire in 1897, he commissioned the British architect **Henry Irwin** to build a new one. The work was completed in 1912, and is a glorious mixture of styles. Within, it seems to owe as much to an Arabian Nights-style fantasy as to the formal Indo-Saracenic school of architecture. There are mosaic floors, silver doors, a solid gold throne weighing 200kg (440lb), and jewel-studded furniture. Gilt and crystal clash with gaudily painted walls and columns. Visit the palace again at nightfall, when the fabulous façade is illuminated by thousands of electric bulbs against a black sky! Open 10:30–17:30, daily (*see* www.mysorepalace.gov.in).

▲ *Above: brightly coloured dye catches the eye in Bengaluru's sprawling Central Market.*

Sri Jayachamarajendra Art Gallery (Jaganmohan Palace) ★

The palace, built in 1861, became an art gallery in 1875. Exhibits include paintings by Indian and foreign artists, portraits of the royal family, and traditional Mysore works in gold leaf. Open 08:00–17:30, daily.

Railway Museum ★

Close to Mysore's splendid railway station (built for the maharajahs) is the **Mysore Railway Museum**, with a collection of locomotives and rolling stock which includes 19th-century carriages from the royal train of the Maharajah of Mysore, as well as an exhibition of historic railway paraphernalia. Open 08:00–17:00, daily.

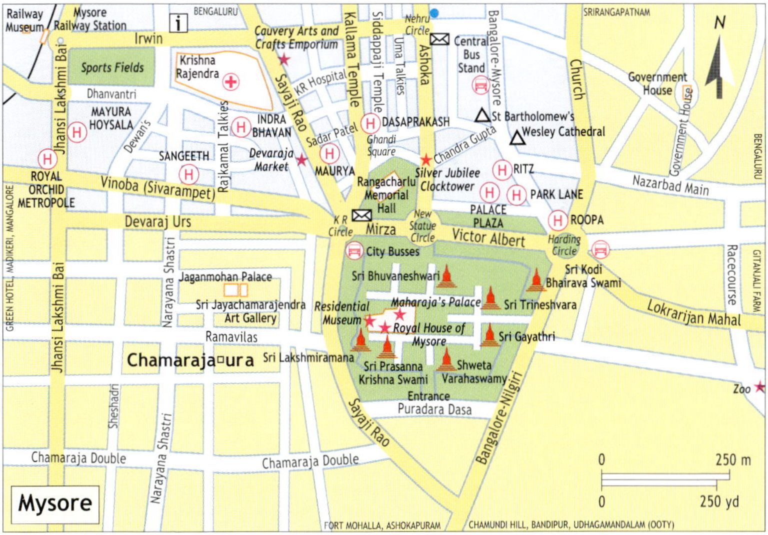

Sandalwood

Mysore is India's incense capital, with the scent of dozens of small incense factories perfuming many city streets. You can visit one of the city's many incense workshops to watch the fragrant sticks and cones being made by hand at terrific speed (enquire at KSTDC information office for details).

▶ *Right: Fishermen enliven the beach scene for tourists at Kovalam.*

Chamundi Hill (Sri Chamundeswari Temple) ★

A thousand steps lead from the foot of this hill, 13km (8 miles) from the city, to the 2000-year-old temple of the Wodeyar dynasty's patron goddess, **Chamundeswari**. Halfway to the top stands a 4.8m (15ft) stone Nandi bull. You can cheat by taking a bus or taxi to the top of the hill.

Sriringapatna (Seringapatam) ★

Situated 16km (10 miles) north of Mysore, this town was the 18th-century capital of the great Muslim leader Hyder Ali Sultan and his son Tipu Sultan, who was killed in battle with the British here in 1799. They endowed the city with a treasury of striking buildings, including Tipu's splendid tomb, the **Gumbaz**, and his summer palace, the **Dariya Daulat** – now a museum with an exhibition of the Sultan's possessions, portraits and weapons. Also worth seeing are the ramparts of Tipu's fort. On an island in the **Cauvery River**, the town was founded by Hindu builders in the 13th century and among its architectural gems is the temple of **Ranganath**.

KERALA

Kerala is one of the smaller states, with a population of around 30 million and a land area of roughly 40,000km^2 (15,500 sq miles). The most widely spoken local language is **Malayalam**. The state shares some of Goa's physical characteristics, forming a ribbon of verdant coastland where coconut palms, cashew nuts and rice are the main crops and many people make their living from fishing. Despite early contacts with the Europeans, however, Kerala did not share Goa's colonial history. It was created within its present borders after independence by merging part of the former province of **Madras** with two princely states, **Cochin** (now Kochi) and **Travancore**, which had been under British sway since the late 18th century. Kerala has the highest literacy rate and the longest life expectancy of any Indian state, but it also has the highest alcohol consumption. In late 2014, the state government moved to ban alcohol and close more than 700 bars and 'toddy shops' where Keralan men gather to drink the local tipple, made from coconut milk. Additional prosperity comes from the United Arab Emirates and other Gulf states, where many local men go to work for high wages (by Indian standards). Bright new cottages built with the earnings of these overseas workers line the coastal highway.

Because of its natural harbour at **Kochi** (Cochin), Kerala has long been exposed to the influence of the world beyond India. It was visited by ancient Greeks and Romans, Jews and Arabs before the arrival of the first Portuguese and

Don't Miss

*** **Kovalam:** the finest beach in Kerala and one of the best in India.
*** **Kochi**: historic city on a spectacular natural harbour.
*** **Kerala backwaters:** delightful boat journey through palm-fringed tropical lagoons.

▲ *Above: Kovalam beach in Kerala is as popular with local people and fishermen as with the tourists who are now discovering it.*

Dutch fleets in the 16th century. Vasco da Gama's first expedition to India in search of 'spices and Christians' found a long-established Christian community, reputedly converted by St Thomas in the 1st century AD.

Fine beaches line Kerala's coast, stretching almost as far as India's southern tip. The state also has a growing tourism industry, with winter-season charter flights from several European airports to **Trivandrum** (Thiruvananthapuram) as well as a growing holiday resort area around **Kovalam**.

Trivandrum and Surrounds ★★

The capital of Kerala state is a pleasant, relaxed city in its own way, with distinctive local architecture and none of the urban pressure associated with most bigger Indian cities. That said, it has no major sight-seeing attractions. The pleasant little **Napier Museum**, close to the city centre, is worth a visit. It has a small collection of bronze statues, carvings and ornate Hindu temple decorations.

For most visitors, the main attraction is the superb beach at **Kovalam**, some 16km (10 miles) south and rapidly becoming a favourite with European package holidaymakers in search of winter sunshine. Like Goa's beaches, Kovalam was an early favourite with low-budget backpackers but the influx of more upmarket tourists has changed its character. There are many new hotels, restaurants and souvenir shops springing up. Kovalam's beaches consist of a chain of three bays separated by a series of headlands.

KOCHI (COCHIN) AND SURROUNDS

A deep natural harbour protected by an array of islands and peninsulas made Kochi one of India's most important cities in ancient times. It was one of the first points of contact between Portugal and India in the early 16th century. A century later, the Dutch ousted the Portuguese, only to be driven out in turn by the British at the beginning of the 18th century during the French Revolutionary Wars.

Each of these colonial powers ruled in alliance with the rajas of the **Varma** dynasty, who remained nominal rulers of Kochi until Independence. Today it remains an economically and strategically vital anchorage for merchant shipping and the Indian navy. The oldest part of the city, **Fort Kochi**, is on the main peninsula south of the harbour mouth. Between it and the more modern city Ernakulam, on the mainland side of the harbour, is the artificial **Willingdon Island**, created from sand dredged out to improve navigation. **Vypeen Island** and **Bolgatty Island**, in the northern half of the bay, are connected to Fort Kochi, Ernakulam and each other by a fleet of ferry-boats and water-taxis.

The trip across the harbour is well worth taking, with fine views of the old and new parts of the port, where container vessels and Indian Navy frigates share the waves with tiny fishing canoes and rice barges. The city's main sightseeing attractions are in **Fort Kochi**, which with its narrow streets, whitewashed buildings and old warehouses and shops, is a great place to wander about. The most attractive part of the old town is **Jew Town**, the area around the historic synagogue.

Kerala Facts and Figures

With a population of over 30 million and a land area of 38,900km^2 (15,015 sq miles), Kerala is one of India's smaller states. Malayalam is the main language, and one in four Keralans is Christian. Fishing and coir fibre manufacture are important local industries and tourism is rapidly becoming a major foreign currency earner.

Christians in Kerala

Kerala's Christians claim to be the first converts in India, having heard the word from **St Thomas**, who is said to have landed in Kerala in 52AD, travelling across southern India to Madras, where he was martyred in 68AD and is reputed to be buried. These earliest Christians were reinforced in later centuries by Christian traders and missionaries from the Middle East, but were then cut off from the rest of Christendom by the Muslim conquests in India.

Chinese Nets ★★★

These wonderful contraptions which line the foreshore at the Fort Kochi side of the harbour mouth were introduced to the region by 14th-century Chinese traders. A gigantic dip-net is suspended from a complex wooden framework some 10m (30ft) high. The weight of the net is balanced out by heavy boulders. Each net is worked by a crew of three or four, and the catch is surprisingly small – a couple of dozen silvery pomfret for each dip of the net. It seems a lot of work for little gain.

Mattancherry Palace (Dutch Palace) ★★★

The original two-storey palace was built by the Portuguese in 1557 in a bid to curry favour with the Raja of Cochin, **Veera Varma** (1537–61). The Dutch, also keen to gain the good graces of the rajas, rebuilt it in the second half of the 17th century. The portraits of the Varma Rajas in the upper gallery show a strong family resemblance, from Rama II Varma (1864–88) to his last inheritor, Rama VII Varma (1948–64). The rajas gave audience seated on a huge platform-swing which is displayed on the first floor along with portraits and ceremonial dress. Some fine murals, depicting scenes from the *Ramayana* and other great Hindu epics, decorate many of the rooms. Leave enough time to examine them in some detail, as each vivid, action-packed section tells a story. Open 08:00–17:00, daily.

▼Below: The small Mattancherry Palace in Kochi contains fine mural paintings of scenes from the Hindu epics.

Paradesi Synagogue ★★

This remarkable building was erected in 1664 on the site of an earlier synagogue by Kochi's long-established Jewish community, the descendants of traders from Palestine who first established links with India almost 2000 years ago. Polished brass pillars support the roof, from which dangle dozens of crystal chandeliers. Open 08:00–17:00, Monday–Thursday.

St Francis Church ★
India's oldest church dates from 1403, when it was built by **Franciscans** who arrived with one of the earliest Portuguese expeditions. There is little to remind the visitor of the building's antecedents, as it has been rebuilt several times, not only by the Portuguese but by their Dutch and British successors.

▲ *Above: Kathakali dancers delight audiences with their elaborate costumes and vivid make-up.*

Bolgatty Palace ★
Bolgatty Island, in the northern half of the bay, was chosen by the Dutch as their headquarters in Kochi. The residence of the Dutch East India Company (VOC) governor on the island was taken over by the British Resident after the Dutch were expelled. Built in 1744, the resident's 'palace' is now an eccentrically run hotel under the control of the Kerala Tourist Development Corporation. There is no denying its character, and it is often used by Mumbai-based film directors looking for a picturesque location. The Bolgatty Palace is also a good place to see **Kathakali**, the thrilling and theatrical traditional dance of Kerala and southern India, in which elaborately costumed and gaudily painted dancers enact scenes from the great Hindu epics (*see* www.bolgattypalacekochi.com).

Periyar Wildlife Sanctuary ★
A century ago, an artificial lake was formed by damming the **Periyar River** in the midst of hill country some 190km (120 miles) east of Kochi. In the 1930s, the lake became the hub of a wildlife sanctuary which now covers some 780km^2 (300 sq miles). Wildlife is viewed by boat from the lake, and while **elephant** and **monkey** may be seen, the shyer animals – including the rare **tiger**, for which the park is one of India's few havens – are often scared into hiding by the noisy boatloads of visitors. The lake attracts a vast number of bird species. If you plan a visit, avoid weekends and Indian holidays, when the reserve is overcrowded and accommodation is usually full.

Kathakali
Kathakali dance re-enacts tales from Indian mythology with dancers (all male) taking the parts of heroes, gods, goddesses and demons. The costumes are elaborate and vividly coloured, as is the make-up. Faces are painted in brilliant swirls of red, green and black, eyes are heavily made up and the whites coloured deep red using aubergine flowers. Each performance is preceded by a brief explanation of the complex gestures and ritualized movements used in the dance-drama.

THE KERALA BACKWATERS

The boat journey through the enchanting Kerala backwaters is one of the main reasons for visiting the state. Fed by numerous streams and rivers flowing out of the eastern mountains, these backwaters are a vast expanse of lagoons and channels pent up behind the sand-bars of the coast. At points along the way, the natural barrier between the fresh-water channel and the open sea is so narrow that you can see the surf beyond it. Dotted with islands and fringed by palm plantations, the backwaters extend 80km (50 miles) or more from **Kollam** in the south to Alappuzha and **Kottayam** in the north, where they connect with the huge, brackish Vembanad Lake which opens into the sea at **Kochi**. Narrow channels and creeks meander from the main back-water lagoons into the countryside around, and tiny villages of fisher-folk and coir (coconut fibre) workers stand on the banks. The silver and green lakes and canals are busy with dozens of boats. They range from waddling, square-rigged rice barges to speedy, gondola-like snake-boats with high-powered outboard motors or tiny circular rafts made out of reeds. The banks are lined with the skeletal gantries of Chinese-style fishing nets.

People of the Backwaters

The people of the Kerala back-waters live by fishing and by growing coconuts for coir, the rough fibre which is made into ropes and matting in Kochi and elsewhere. Fishing may be from boats or rafts or from the shore using the Chinese style nets which are also to be seen on the waterfront. Coconuts are husked and stacked neatly along the water's edge for collection by boat.

It is possible to make an extensive two- to three-day boat journey from Kochi to Kollam, but most people opt for the six- to eight-hour trip between Kollam and Alappuzha or the shorter two- to three-hour journey between Alappuzha and Kottayam. Several boats leave daily in each direction, operated by either the Kerala Tourist Development Corporation, local municipalities or some private operators. Tourist boats carry around 30 passengers even though the cabins and decks are rather small. They usually stop for lunch at one of the small villages en route and later tourists can have a swim in the lake.

▲ *Above: Heavy-laden rice barges make their slow way under sail through the backwater channels and lagoons.*
◀ *Opposite: Paddle-powered for a traditional race, snakeboats have outboard motors for everyday use.*

Kollam (Quilon)

Kollam is the southern jumping-off point for the backwaters, located about 120km (75 miles) south of Kochi. Close to the mouth of **Ashtamudi Lake**, which opens into the sea, Kollam itself is a place of no great interest, though there is an adequate beach at **Thangasseri**, 3km (2 miles) southeast of town.

Alappuzha (Alleppey)

Alappuzha, 45km (30 miles) south of Kochi, is a small but lively town criss-crossed by canals which link the northern channels of the backwaters with the southern end of **Vembanad Lake**. It is the northern terminus for the backwater trip. Boats also run through the canals to Vembanad Lake and Kottayam which is a picturesque shorter journey of roughly three hours. Real boat-travel fans can also continue to Kochi and Ernakulam via the lake.

Kottayam

Kottayam, the third gateway to the backwaters, is about 25km (15 miles) east of Alappuzha, and is linked with Vembanad Lake by its own system of waterways. Though of historic interest – St Thomas is said to have made converts here early in the Christian era – it offers no exciting sightseeing.

Spices

Kerala produces most of the spices which combine to create Indian cuisine's piquant flavours. Most of India's **pepper**, 60% of its **cardamom** and almost all of its **ginger** – in fact, most of the world's ginger – is grown here. **Nutmeg** and **chillis** are also grown on the Kerala plantations.

KARNATAKA AND KERALA AT A GLANCE

Best Times to Visit

Karnataka is perfect to visit from **November** to **February**, with daytime temperatures of 26°C to 30°C (79°F to 86°F) and low rainfall. **March** to **May** is uncomfortably hot and dusty. Rains begin in June–July and are at their heaviest in October.

Getting There

Bengaluru: Two to three buses daily from Bijapur (8 hours), Mumbai (24 hours or more), Ernakulam (10 hours); and 15 buses daily from Mysore (four hours). Several trains run daily from Mumbai, Bijapur, Hampi, Mysore and all points in central and southern India. One train runs daily from Vasco. Flights from Goa, Mumbai and all major Indian cities. **Hampi:** buses and trains are available from Goa, Vasco and Bengaluru. **Bijapur:** buses from Hampi (4 hours) and Bengaluru (8 hours). Trains also available from Hampi and Bengaluru. Frequent buses connect **Aihole**, **Pattadakal** and **Badami**. Badami is the best point for onward travel connections, with a daily bus (4 hours) and six trains (3½ hours) to Bijapur to the north and Hampi. The three sites can be explored by local bus, but for those with more money to spend, the best is to take a taxi from Badami railway station. For travel to Mysore, buses and trains go from Bengaluru and Kochi or Ernakulam (6 hours). To get to **Trivandrum** take a bus from Kochi (6 hours). Flights from Mumbai (2 hours, 30 mins) and Bengaluru (1 hour, 30 mins), and international charter flights (12–13 hours) from various European airports. There are buses (8 hours) and trains from Bengaluru to **Kochi**. Daily flights from Bengaluru (1 hour), Trivandrum (30 mins) and several times daily to Mumbai (two hours, 30 min). Several trains and buses travel daily from Kochi (3–4 hours) and Trivandrum (1–2 hours) to **Kollam**. Buses and daily boats via the backwaters to **Alappuzha**. Frequent buses (2–3 hours) from Kollam and Kochi. To Alappuzha, several trains daily (1–2 hours) from Ernakulam. Package-tour passengers arriving at Trivandrum international airport are met by couriers and transfer coaches to get to **Kottayam**. For independent travellers, there are buses half-hourly from Trivandrum, taking less than 30 mins. Other options between Kottayam and Trivandrum include taxis and auto-rickshaws. The Konkan Railway connects Mumbai and Goa with Ernakulam (Cochin) and points between.

Getting Around

Bengaluru: taxis and auto-rickshaws within the city limits; taxis run to points outside the city limits. Car hire with driver available from major hotels.
Kochi/Ernakulam: Taxis and auto-rickshaws on land. Ferry network connects Ernakulam with Fort Kochi, Bolgatty and other islands. Hire a motorboat from the pier on the mainland opposite the Bolgatty Palace.
Mysore: Taxis, auto-rickshaws or car hire with driver from main hotels and tour agencies.

Where to Stay

Bengaluru

Luxury

Vivanta by Taj, 41/3 Mahatma Gandhi Road, tel: 08066 604 444, www.vivantabytaj.com
The Oberoi Bangalore, 37–39 Mahatma Gandhi Road, tel: 08025 585 858, www.oberoibangalore.com Exceptional hotel.

Mid-range

Villa Pottipatti, 142 4th Main Road, Crossroad 8, Malleswaram, Bengaluru, tel: 08023 360 777, www.neemranahotels.com Heritage property, recently restored with all mod cons (including Internet access in every room), set among gardens on the edge of Bengaluru's 'Silicon City'. Superb value.

Bijapur

Budget

Hotel Mayura Adil Shahi, Anand Mahal Road, tel: 0835 225 0401. Comfortable, cheap hotel run by the **Karnataka State Tourism Development Corporation**. The annex has better rooms and is quieter.

Mysore

Luxury

Royal Orchid Hotel, 5 Jhansi-Lakshmibai Road, Chamundi Hills, tel: 08214 520 690, www.royalorchidhotels.com Splendid classic hotel, recently refurbished to luxury standards but retains plenty of character.

Mid-range/Budget

Gitanjali Homestay, Siddarthanagar, Mysore, tel: 0821 247 4646, www.gitanjalihomestay.com Tiny family-run guesthouse just outside Mysore. Full board only but wonderful food.

Green Hotel, Chittaranjan Palace, 2270 Vinoba (Hunsur) Road, Jayalakshmipuram, tel: 08214 255 000, www.greenhotelindia.com Superb restored palace, among formal lawns. Best in Mysore.

Trivandrum

Most accommodation is in family homes, guesthouses or in new package-holiday hotels.

Luxury

Travancore Heritage, Chowara, Trivandrum, tel: 0471 226 7828, www.thetravancoreheritage.com Made from traditional Kerala houses. Offers Ayurvedic health treatments.

Kochi

Luxury

Malabar House, 1/268 Parade Road, Fort Kochi, tel: 04842 381 038, www.malabarhouse.com Magical boutique hotel. Best place to stay in Kerala.

Brunton Boatyard, Fort Kochi, tel: 04842 215 462, www.cghearth.com Boutique hotel on Kochi's natural harbour.

Mid-range

Metropolitan, South Railway Station, Cochin, tel: 04842 375 285, www.metropolitancochin.com Modern hotel with air-conditioned rooms.

Budget

Fort House tel: 04842 217 103, www.hotelforthouse.com On the edge of the grand harbour. Combines simple but immaculately clean rooms, a great restaurant and fine view. Highly recommended.

Periyar

Luxury

Shalimar Spice Garden, Murikaddy, Idukki District, Kerala, tel: 04869 222 2132, fax: 222 3022, www.shalimarkerala.net Lovely, relaxing rustic retreat near the Periyar Wildlife Sanctuary.

Where to Eat

Outside the larger cities, eateries are basic and the most reliable restaurants are in hotels.

Bengaluru

A good selection of restaurants serving Asian and international cuisine. Outside main hotels (most offer a choice of European, Indian, Chinese or Japanese cuisine) there is still plenty of choice. Church Street offers a range, including **Coconut Grove**, with open-air tables, south Indian meals and draught beer, and **Tavern at the Inn** and the **Museum Inn**, offering an Indian take on the traditional English pub, with beer and bar snacks.

Mysore

Best value is the barbecue on the lawn at **Hotel Metropole**, which also has a fine restaurant indoors. The **Hotel Durbar** is good value and its rooftop restaurant overlooks the park.

Trivandrum

Hotel restaurants are mediocre, but small restaurant shacks offer excellent value, especially for seafood. Drinks are expensive. These restaurants close from June to September.

Kochi/Ernakulam

The classiest place to eat is Taj Malabar's waterfront terrace.

Tours and Excursions

Kerala Travels, MM Church Building, Museum Junction, Trivandrum, tel: 0471 272 7478; Kochi office, tel: 0484 401 0403; Bengaluru office, tel: 08411 121 546, www.keralatravels.com operates tours throughout southern India.

Useful contacts

Kerala Tourism, Park View, Trivandrum, tel: 0471 232 1132, www.ktdc.com

Karnataka Tourism, 49 2nd Floor, Khanija Bhavan, Race Course Road, Bengaluru, tel: 080 235 2828, www.karnataka.com

8
Highlights of Maharashtra

Maharashtra, the state north of Goa, is one of the largest in India and offers huge contrasts. Its capital, **Mumbai**, is for many the gateway to India. From the 17th century, it was the heartland of the Maratha empire, whose Hindu rulers successfully defied the power of the **Mughal** empire. The state is consequently dotted with the forts and castles of Maratha rulers. Among the important sightseeing attractions are Maharashtra's many cave temples, cut into the rock by earlier Buddhist, Jain and Hindu dwellers in the region. The most dramatic, at **Ajanta** and **Ellora**, rank among the world's most stunning ancient religious sites.

Maharashtra's Arabian Sea coast rises to the continental chain of the **Western Ghats** and the arid **Deccan** plateau. Travelling within the state is comparatively easy, with frequent air services between Mumbai and places of interest, fast and comfortable express trains on key routes, and a good road network. During the British colonial era, hill stations of Maharashtra's mountain country were developed to provide the *sahibs* with relief from the summer heat of Mumbai. Of these, **Pune** (Poona), **Mahabaleshwar** and **Matheran** are pleasantly temperate compared with the coastal regions of Maharashtra .

Today, the state is an economic powerhouse, due to Mumbai's thriving heavy and service industries and its huge import and export sector. As elsewhere in India, however, outside Maharashtra's bigger industrial cities rural life continues more or less untouched.

Don't Miss

*** **Ellora:** complex of magnificently carved rock temples, more than a thousand years old.
*** **Ajanta:** more ancient cave temples, superbly decorated with frescoes and Buddha images.
** **Daulatabad:** grim hilltop fortress built more than six centuries ago. Awesome fortifications and spectacular location.

◀ *Opposite: Carved Buddha images guard the entrance to the Ajanta cave temple complex in Maharashtra.*

HIGHLIGHTS OF MAHARASHTRA

Sivaji

Maharashtra was the stamping ground of the **Marathas**, a warlike Hindu people who emerged in the 17th century as a focus of resistance against Muslim encroachment. Their first and greatest ruler, Sivaji, successfully defied the Mughals of Delhi and created an independent Maratha kingdom. After his death this kingdom became a confederacy of Maratha princes, headed by a hereditary Peshwa with his seat in Pune. They remained a great Indian power until their final defeat by the British in 1818.

AURANGABAD AND SURROUNDS

The main reason for visiting this city of 600,000, some 320km (200 miles) east of Mumbai, is to see the wonderful cave temples at **Ajanta** and **Ellora** and the great Mughal stronghold at **Daulatabad**. Aurangabad also has some less distinguished cave temples of its own.

Aurangabad Caves ★

About 4km (2½ miles) from the city centre and roughly 1km (⅔ miles) apart stand two groups of cave temples. They date from the later **Buddhist** era, and were built around the 7th century AD. The eastern caves, with their carved Buddha images, demigods and demons, are the most interesting.

Daulatabad ★★

The fortress of Daulatabad stands about 16km (10 miles) west of Aurangabad. The complex hilltop fortifications date from the 1320s, when the Sultan of Delhi, known as **Mohammed bin Tughlaq**, attempted to relocate his capital here, forcing the inhabitants of Delhi to move to the new site. The plan failed, and Daulatabad became a ghost fortress.

Ellora ★★★

The Ellora cave complex, about 30km (18 miles) northwest of Aurangabad, covers a 2km (1¼ miles) section of hillside and includes Buddhist, Hindu and Jain temples. The original complex comprises 34 caves, of which half are Hindu works, dating from the 9th century to the 13th century. A second cave complex, in the hills above Ellora, was found in 1990 and is being excavated. By far the most striking of them is the vast **Kailasha Temple**, the largest monolithic building in the world, elaborately carved with scenes from the **Mahabharata**, **Ramayana** and other Hindu epics. Other caves with finely preserved friezes include the Ramesvara, Dumar Lena and Das Avatara. Five **Jain rock temples** on the north side of the site are also worth looking at for their delicate sculptures.

Maharashtra's Masses

With a population of more than 80 million, Maharashtra is one of India's most crowded states. More than 10% of its population is concentrated in the sprawling metropolis of Mumbai, which continues to draw in immigrants from the countryside. The semi-arid Deccan plateau occupies much of the state.

◀ *Left: Frescoes of the Buddha and his disciples illustrate the oldest buddhist cave temples in India, at Ajanta.*

The Pune Ashram

The man who did most to put Pune on the world map in the 1970s was **Bhagwan Rajneesh**, or **Osho**, as he later preferred to be called, who located the *ashram* (retreat) of his personal cult in the city. One of several Indian gurus who gained a worldwide following in the hippy era, Bhagwan advocated laughter, tears and sex as routes to enlightenment. He died in 1990, but his cult still seems to attract a steady trickle of devotees from Europe, the USA and Japan.

Ajanta ★★★

The **Buddhist cave temples** at Ajanta, 100km (62 miles) northeast of Aurangabad, are among the oldest in India. They date from as early as the 2nd century BC when Buddhist monks settled here to begin the work of carving temples and sanctuaries from the walls of this rocky gorge. They were abandoned during the 7th century AD and rediscovered in 1819. The caves are decorated with **carvings** and gigantic **Buddha images**. The superb murals, painted in red, black, yellow and blue, depict scenes from the life of the Buddha and his disciples, and are even finer than the carvings.

PUNE (POONA) AND SURROUNDS

Now a busy modern city, Pune was a popular refuge from the Mumbai heat during the British colonial era and still attracts people from Mumbai, especially during the monsoon season. Pune also received worldwide recognition as it was the headquarters of the **Sri Bhagwan Rajneesh** cult during the 1970s and '80s.

▼ Below: Maharashtra women are traditionally among the most colourfully clad in India.

The 8th-century **Panchaleshwar Rock Temple** is similar to those at Ellora but is smaller and less impressive than its neighbours.

A splendidly eclectic private collection of artifacts and artworks, at the **Raja Kelkar Museum**, includes Hindu miniature paintings, arms and armour, musical instruments and furniture.

The wonderful 6ha (15-acre) **Gandhi National Memorial** garden surrounds the tomb of Kasturba Gandhi, the wife of India's great independence leader, who died here in 1944 while interned by the British. The Gandhis and other leaders of the 'Quit India' movement were interned in the former palace of the Aga Khan, which was given to the Indian government in 1969.

Best Times to Visit

The more pleasant months in Maharashtra are from **December** through to **March**, when rainfall is minimal and the maximum daytime temperatures are around 30°C (86°F). Avoid the hot, dry months of April and May, and also the monsoon months of June to mid-October. Rainfall is heaviest in June and July, when there are daily downpours.

Getting There

There are daily **flights** to **Aurangabad** from Mumbai. The flights last approximately one hour. There are also flights between Mumbai and Pune. **Buses** are also available from Mumbai (the journey takes about 10 hours) as well as from Pune (roughly five hours). Frequent buses are available to **Daulatabad** from Aurangabad which will take about 30 minutes. Buses leave hourly from Aurangabad to the **Ajanta Caves** (three hours). There are half-hourly buses from Aurangabad to the **Ellora Caves** which is roughly a 30-minute trip. There are several **flights** daily to Bengaluru from Mumbai, **Pune** and Chennai. Several **trains** arrive daily from Mumbai – the journey may last between three and five hours – and from Bengaluru (31 hours).

Getting Around

You can hire taxis and **auto-rickshaws** in both Aurangabad and Pune. **Cars** with a driver can be hired by the day from larger hotels and from the **Maharashtra State Tourism Development Corporation**. In Pune, **bicycles** are available for rent at several of the smaller hotels.

Where to Stay

Aurangabad

Luxury

Ajanta Ambassador Hotel, Chikal Than, tel: 0240 248 5211, www.ambassadorindia.com Good value for money. Has a pool.

Welcomgroup Rama International, Rajendra Prasad Marg, tel: 0240 663 4141, www.welcomhotelrama.com Top hotel.

Pune

Luxury

Taj Blue Diamond, 11 Koregaon Road, tel: 0202 660 2555, www.vivantabytaj.com This is the top hotel in Pune, with all the luxury trimmings, located in the newest part of the city.

Mid-range

Hotel Aurora Towers, 9 Moledina Road, tel: 0202 613 1818, www.hotelauroratowers.com Good hotel in Pune.

Hotel Sagar Plaza, 1 Bund Garden Road, tel: 0206 205 0000, www.hotelsagarplaza.com Recently built. Has a pool.

Where to Eat

Aurangabad

Outside hotels, eating places are rather basic and mediocre. The **Ajanta Ambassador's restaurants** are highly recommended.

Pune

Moledina Road is lined with restaurants offering Indian cuisine, burgers and international menus.

For up-market dining, the **Aurora Towers Hotel** has a choice of international, Indian and Chinese cuisine.

Tours and Excursions

The **Maharashtra Tourism Development Corporation** (*see* Useful Contacts) operates excursions from Mumbai to all the destinations and major sights. Destinations include the Ellora and Ajanta cave temples.

Useful Contacts

India Tourist Development Corporation, 123 Maharishi Karve Road, Mumbai, tel: 022 203 3144/45.

Maharashtra Tourism Development Corporation, 9th Floor, Express Towers, Nariman Point, Mumbai, tel: 022 202 4482, www.maharashtratourism.gov.in

Travel Tips

Tourist Information

India Tourism (www.incredibleindia.org) handles all overseas information.

Within India:

Maharashtra Tourism, 9th Floor, Nariman Point, Mumbai 400 021, tel: 00 91 22 202 4482, fax: 00 91 22 202 4521, www.maharashtratourism.gov.in

Goa Dept. of Tourism, Patto, Panaji, Goa 403001, tel: 00 91 832 243 8750, fax: 00 91 832 243 8756, www.goa-tourism.com

Karnataka Tourism, 2nd Floor, Khanija Bhavan, Race Course Road, Bengaluru 560 001, tel: 00 91 80 235 2828, fax: 00 91 80 235 2626, www.karnatakatourism.org

Kerala Tourism, Yatri Nivas, Thycaud, Trivandrum 695014, tel: 00 91 471 232 7262, fax: 00 91 471 232 7265, www.keralatourism.org

Entry Requirements

All visitors require a visa. Tourist visas are normally valid for up to six months from date of issue. Visa forms can be completed online (www.indianvisaonline.gov.in), but applicants must still appear in person at the relevant high commission, embassy or consulate for interview and provide proof that they have a return ticket and enough funds to cover their entire stay.

Indian Embassies, Consulates and High Commissions:

UK: India House, Aldwych, London WC2B 4NA, tel: 0171 836 0990, www.hcilondon.in

USA: 2107 Massachusetts Avenue, Washington DC 20008, tel: 202 939 7000, www.indianembassy.org

Australia: 3–5 Moonah Place, Yarralula, ACT 2600, tel: 06 273 3999.

Canada: 10 Springfield Road, Ottawa, K1M 1C9, tel: 613 744 3751, www.hciottawa.ca

South Africa: 52 Schoeman Street, Arcadia 0083, Pretoria, tel: 012 34 5310, www.hcipretoria.za

Customs

You may import one litre of spirits or wine and 200 cigarettes. Hi-tech equipment such as video cameras or notebook computers should be registered on a tourist re-export form.

Health Requirements

Immunization against cholera, typhoid, polio, meningitis, hepatitis A and tetanus is strongly advisable. Take medical advice before travelling. Malaria is prevalent and a course of malaria prophylactics is essential. Take a good supply of mosquito repellent. Do not drink water unless it has been boiled and use water purifying tablets. Comprehensive health and accident insurance is essential.

Getting There

Ebola screening was introduced at some airports for arrivals from Africa in late 2014.

By Air: Main gateways for scheduled flights from Europe and North America are Mumbai, New Delhi, Bengaluru and Chennai, with daily flights by Air India and other major airlines from most European capitals and from North America. The flight time from London is around 11 hours, and about 19 hours from New York. Air India and many other national carriers also connect Mumbai and New Delhi with major cities in Australasia and Asia. Qatar Airlines flies to Kochi in Kerala with connections from Glasgow, to London, Manchester and other European cities via Doha. Direct charter flights to Goa and to Trivandrum operate from London and several major European airports during the tourist high season (Sept–Apr).

By Road: Long-distance buses connect Goa with Mumbai, Bengaluru, Mysore and other points in Karnataka and Maharashtra states. (Long-haul bus travel can be rather arduous.)

By Rail: The Konkan Railway connects Goa with Mumbai and several stations en route and continues south into Karnataka. Express trains also connect Goa Vasco da Gama station with Bengaluru and Mysore. For Indian Rail tickets, Indrail passes and luxury trains including the Golden Chariot journey (Goa to Bengaluru), the official UK sales agent is SD Enterprises, tel: 0208 903 3411, www.indiarail.co.uk

By Boat: When this edition was updated there was no service by sea to Goa. However, ferries between Mumbai and Goa were reportedly due to start operating in 2015.

What to Pack

Take the minimum amount of clothing for a Goan beach holiday. Shorts and T-shirts are all you will need at beach resorts. More modest clothing is required for sightseeing, visits to temples and churches, and any travel away from the beach.

Money Matters

The Indian rupee is divided into 100 paisa. When this edition was updated for 2015, the rupee was valued at approximately Rs96= UK£1, Rs 60= US$1 and Rs77= €1. Currency can be **exchanged** at banks in main cities and at your hotel. Retain currency conversion slips to reconvert rupees on your departure. ATM cash machines are available in major cities, towns and some resorts but there may be a charge for withdrawals using credit or debit cards. Credit cards are not widely accepted outside major hotels. When changing money, ask for some low-denomination notes and coins as rickshaw and taxi drivers often deny having change for larger notes. Be aware that any note that is torn, dirty or defaced may be refused as payment. **Tipping** is universal for all services, but there is no set percentage and a very small tip of a few rupees will usually suffice.

Accommodation

Goa and other tourist centres offer a wide range of accommodation, from extremely basic guesthouses catering to budget travellers to five-star luxury resorts and business hotels. Top range hotels in India are surprisingly cheap by international standards. While facilities match international levels, service standards may be more relaxed. Off the beaten track, accommodation can be extremely substandard, though also extremely cheap.

Road Signs

Self drive car hire is not advisable in India, but be aware that sometimes the signposting is rather poor on Indian roads and may pose problems. Street names and shop signs are luckily almost always in English, as are railway station name-signs, platform indicators and timetables.

Eating Out

Eating out has become both affordable and fashionable for India's new middle class and is no longer just for tourists. Mumbai is replete with places to eat, as are (to a a lesser extent) Bengaluru and Kochi. In Goa, tiny, simple thatched restaurants line every beach, closing during the monsoon (when they are often partially demolished by high seas) to re-open with the beginning of the new tourist season. Don't expect a wide or sophisticated menu, though a choice of simpler international standards – such as burgers, steak and omelettes – is usually on offer along with spicy local seafood. Five-star hotels in major cities usually offer a choice of two or three restaurants – usually a coffee shop serving international meals, one or more restaurants serving traditional regional cuisine, as well as a Chinese or Japanese restaurant. Small cafés, often called hotels, cater to Indian workers and travellers. The menu in these is usually very simple and meals are extremely cheap. A *thali*, a plated meal consisting of various kinds of *dal* (lentil) dishes, spicy vegetable dips, curds and yoghurt, is one of the best meals to order.

Beer and **wine** are luxury drinks in India, affordable only by the relatively wealthy, and most small cafés and restaurants which cater to ordinary Indians do not serve alcohol.

Transport

Air: The national carrier Indian Airlines operates a number of domestic routes in competition with several privately owned airlines. These include Jet Airways (www.jetairways.com), IndiGo (www.book.goindigo.in), Spicejet (www.spicejet.com), JetKonnect (www.jetkonnect.com) and GoAir (www.goair.in). All can be booked online or by phone, but it be easier to book using a local travel agency or the travel desk at your hotel. Fares are very affordable by international standards.

Trains: India's rail network is one of the world's largest. The **class** system is complicated, comprising air conditioned (A/C) and non A/C 1st class, A/C sleeper and chair car, 2nd class sleeper, reserved-seat 2nd class, and unreserved 2nd class. Fares are very cheap. Unreserved 2nd class is always incredibly crowded and should be avoided wherever possible. Rail travel can be **booked** via a hotel, tour agency or at Indian Railways computerized booking offices, found in the departure hall of even the small main stations or online at www.indianrail.gov.in The Indrail Pass, sold by Indian Railways, allows travel on any train for periods of 24 hours, and 7, 15, 30, 60 or 90 days. It is sold by sales agents worldwide. Mumbai has two long-distance railway stations. Central Railways trains go not from Central Station but from **Victoria Terminus** close to the Fort area of town, which handles trains to Karnataka, Maharashtra and onward connections to Goa, as well as services to Madhya Pradesh, Uttar Pradesh, Haryana, and Rajasthan. **Central Station**, north of the city centre, handles Western Railway services to Agra and New Delhi, Rajasthan and Gujarat. Vasco da Gama is the main station for Goa, with rail connections only to Karnataka. The Konkan Railway, completed in 1998, connects Goa with the Maharashtra coast to the north and the Karnataka coast to the south. Aurangabad, Pune, Bijapur, Bengaluru, Mysore, Kochi, Kollam and Trivandrum all have mainline rail services.

Buses: Long distance buses link Goa with all the surrounding states. Fares are very low, but so are standards of comfort. Bus travel should be a last resort.

Taxis: Ordinary taxis are black with a yellow roof. Theoretically they are metered, but the appearance of a foreigner frequently causes mysterious meter malfunctions. Insist on the meter, agree a fare before boarding, or find another driver.

Auto-rickshaws: Hybrids of motor-scooter and chariot, with a bench-seat for two mounted behind the driver and partially enclosed by a canopy. Like taxis, they are supposed to be metered but fares are almost always a matter of haggling. In many places, 'auto' drivers speak

Conversion Chart

From	To	Multiply By
Millimetres	Inches	0.0394
Metres	Yards	1.0936
Metres	Feet	3.281
Kilometres	Miles	0.6214
Square kilometres	Square miles	0.386
Hectares	Acres	2.471
Litres	Pints	1.760
Kilograms	Pounds	2.205
Tonnes	Tons	0.984

To convert Celsius to Fahrenheit: x 9 ÷ 5 + 32

very little English.
Car hire: Self-drive car hire is not recommended because of the many peculiar hazards of Indian motoring. Cars with drivers can be hired by the day from top hotels, travel agencies, TDC offices and car rental outlets.
Motorcycles: Motorcycles can be hired in several of the Goan beach resorts. Maintenance and safety standards are somewhat shaky and crash helmets are not usually provided. Do not rent a motorcycle unless you are familiar with motorbikes and also have a sound mechanical knowledge.

Business Hours

Banks open from 10:00–14:00, Monday–Friday and 10:00–12:00, Saturday. Post offices open from 10:00–17:00, weekdays and 10:00–12:00, Saturdays. Many **shops** in Goa close from around midday until late afternoon. Because of its many different faiths, India has a huge calendar of regional and national religious festivals, during which most shops and offices are closed.

Time Difference

GMT + 5 hrs 30 mins.

Communications

Indian **postal** services are slow but reliable. Most holiday hotels sell stamps. International direct-dial **phone** and **fax** facilities can be found in most holiday hotels. However, vast numbers of Indians prefer to use **mobile phones**, and mobile phone (cellphone) coverage in Mumbai and most of Goa is adequate. You can keep call costs down by buying a local, pay as you go SIM card which can be topped up as needed. There are numerous shops selling these in cities, towns and even villages throughout India. **Internet** access is widely available in Mumbai and in most of Goa, with many hotels and bars offering free WiFi connection. The number for Directory Enquiries is 191 and the international code for India is 00 91.

Electricity

Normally three-pin round sockets (unique to India), 230–240 volts AC. Many Goa establishments use European-style two-pin sockets. Most hotels can provide adaptors for UK, US and EU standard plugs.

Weights & Measures

India uses the metric system of weights and measures.

Health Precautions

It is essential that you take comprehensive health precautions and medical advice before travelling to India and many inoculations must be administered several weeks before departure. Comprehensive medical **insurance**, which should include emergency repatriation, is a must. Do not drink **tap water** in India unless you have boiled or sterilized it yourself. Carry water sterilizing tablets, available from chemists in the UK and elsewhere, and a water bottle if you are heading off the beaten track where bottled drinks may not be available. Food is not guaranteed to be safe anywhere in India, even in luxury hotels. In general, you just have to trust your own judgement as to whether a restaurant looks acceptably clean. Many travellers choose to avoid meat completely in India, and cooked vegetarian food

Public Holidays and Festivals

6 January •
Reis Magos, Feast of the Three Kings, Christian festival
26 January •
Republic Day
Second Sunday after Easter •
Feast of Our Lady of Miracles
13 June •
Feast of St Anthony
24 June •
Feast of St John the Baptist
29 June •
Festival of St Peter
August •
Krishna's birthday
15 August •
Independence Day
21–24 August •
Harvest festival
2 October •
Mahatma Gandhi's birthday
October/early November •
Divali, the Hindu New Year and Festival of Lights, celebrated with fireworks, lanterns and parades
25 December •
Christmas Day

Good Reading

- Mehta, Suketu (2004) *Maximum City: Bombay Lost and Found.*
- Roberts, Gregory David (2005) *Shantaram.*
- Mistry, Rohinton (2006) *A Fine Balance.*
- Chandra, Vikram (2006) *Sacred Games.*
- De Luna, Marissa (2011) *Goa Traffic.*
- Thayil, Jeet Narcopolis (2013)
- Potter, Alexandra (2014) *The Love Detective.*
- Boo, Katherine (2014) *Behind the Beautiful Forevers.*
- Tomory, David (2000) *Hello Goodnight: A Life of Goa.*

may pose fewer health risks. **Malaria** is present in southern India. Your doctor will prescribe the appropriate prophylactics, but the best way to avoid malaria is to avoid being bitten by mosquitoes. A repellent containing a high percentage of *deet*, diethyltoluamide, can be applied to skin, hair or clothing and is effective. Mosquito nets can be bought in specialist travel shops abroad or on arrival in India. **Sunburn** and heat exhaustion are significant risks. Minimize time spent in the sun and cover up. Take plenty of non-alcoholic fluids to avoid dehydration. Beware of infection in small cuts and scrapes: wash carefully and apply an antiseptic ointment or cream.

Health Services

Most five-star hotels have a doctor on call. In emergencies, private clinics offer a faster response than general hospitals. Your insurance must include an emergency repatriation option.

Personal Safety

Incidents of violent crime are very rare but **theft** is not uncommon. Do not leave passports, cash, travellers cheques, travel documents or other valuables in your room. Carry them with you or put them in the hotel safe. Possessions left unattended on the beach are especially vulnerable. Keep a close watch on your possessions when travelling by train. Reporting theft to the police is a time-consuming bureaucratic process. The use of soft drugs, especially marijuana, is widespread among young budget travellers to Goa. The Indian authorities believe that drug use can be stamped out by imposing severe penalties, including 10-year jail sentences, for possession of even small amounts. You may possibly be approached by drug dealers. Be cautious and aware that many of them double as police informers or may even be plainclothes policemen.

Emergencies

Ambulance: 102
Fire: 101
Police: 100
Single emergency number: 108

Etiquette

Indians value modesty. Beachwear is acceptable at beach resorts, far less acceptable elsewhere, and wholly unacceptable in churches, mosques, temples and national monuments. Remove your shoes on entering places of worship. If you are travelling on business, jacket and tie for men and formal business attire for women are the norm; even if you are on holiday, you will find dealing with Indian officialdom (in post offices, police stations, railway booking offices and other situations) easier if you are less informally dressed. Topless sunbathing and nudity are tolerated on some Goan beaches, but arouse intense curiosity among Indian visitors.

Language

India is a land of many different languages. There are 15 major languages as well as hundreds of dialects. Although Hindi is the official national language, it is not really that widely spoken in southern India. Throughout India, English is spoken everywhere: in shops, offices and hotels and by almost all educated Indians.

INDEX
Note: Numbers in **bold** indicate photographs

INDEX

PLACE NAMES IN INDIA

Some of the names of places in India have recently, or over recent years, been changed back to their original Indian names. The following list gives the previous and current names of the main places affected in this book. The names adopted in the book are marked below with an asterisk.

Previous Name	Current Name
Bangalore	Bengaluru*
Bombay	Mumbai*
Calicut*	Kozhikode
Cochin	Kochi*
Panjim	Panaji*
Poona	Pune*
Quilon	Kollam*
Trivandrum*	Thiruvanathapuram
Victoria Terminus* (Mumbai)	Chatrapati Shivaji Maharaj Terminus